LOST BONANZAS
Of Western Canada

Edited By
GARNET BASQUE

Heritage House

CANADIAN CATALOGUING IN PUBLICATION DATA

Main entry under title:

Lost Bonanzas of Western Canada

First ed. by T.W. Paterson.
Includes index.
Bibliography: p. 158
ISBN 1-895811-40-6

1. Treasure-trove—Northwest, Canadian. 2. Northwest, Canadian—History,
local. I. Basque, Garnet. II. Paterson, T.W.
(Thomas William), 1943-   Lost bonanzas of Western Canada
FC3206.P38 1988   971.05   C88-091556-0
F1060.P38 1988

Printing History: **Sunfire Edition**   **Heritage House Edition**
First printing—1983   Fourth printing—1996
Second printing: revised—1988   Fifth printing—2000
Third printing: full colour edition—1990

Heritage House wishes to acknowledge the financial support of the Government
of Canada and Heritage Canada through the Book Publishing Industry Development
Program, and of the British Columbia Arts Council. Thanks also to the staff of the
British Columbia Archives and Records Service (BCARS).

Design, layout and maps by Garnet Basque

HERITAGE HOUSE PUBLISHING COMPANY LTD.
Unit #108 - 17655 66 A Ave., Surrey, BC V3S 2A7

Printed in Hong Kong

Photo Credits
Joe Adams: 116. Garnet Basque: 9, 13 (bottom), 20, 21, 50, 53, 54, 65 (bottom),
68, 72, 74 (bottom), 80, 85 (main), 92 (main), 96, 97, 104 (main), 112, 128, 132.
B.C. Archives and Records Service: 10, 25 (top left and bottom), 28, 40, 44
(bottom), 62, 65 (top), 74 (top), 81 (centre and bottom), 85 (inset), 89, 104 (inset),
108, 122, 125, 141. R. Candy: 81 (top). Environment Canada: 136 (inset), 144,
145, 148, 152. Paul Grignon: 16. Eric Jamieson: 25 (top right), 32. Bill Maximick:
13 (top). Montana Historical Society: 121 (bottom), 138 (bottom). Public Archives
of Canada: 121 (top). Sunfire Archives: Front cover, 24, 44 (top left and right), 67,
92 (inset), 138 (top). J.H. Wilson: 76. Yukon Archives: 136 (main).

CONTENTS

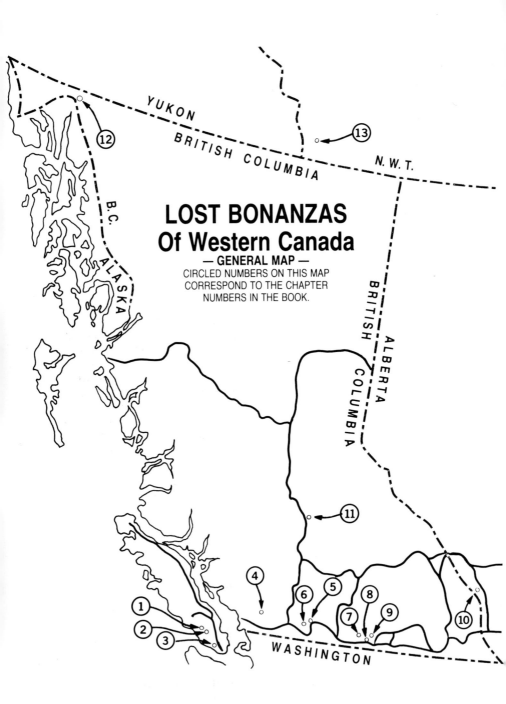

LOST BONANZAS
Of Western Canada
— GENERAL MAP —
CIRCLED NUMBERS ON THIS MAP
CORRESPOND TO THE CHAPTER
NUMBERS IN THE BOOK.

INTRODUCTION

TREASURE! Next to gold, this is probably the single most magical word in the English language. The very mention of the word stirs the adventuresome spirit in most of us. But why are we so fascinated with tales of lost, sunken or buried treasure? Why, like little children, are we so captivated by the tenuous hopes of discovering a treasure which, as adults, we know probably does not exist? Is it the adventure? Is it the escapism to a different place and time? Is it the eternal hope that the treasure just might exist, and we might be the lucky one to discover it? The answer is probably a combination of all these factors, plus the fact that treasures are occasionally found and highly publicized.

Fifteen years ago, while visiting the ghost town of Granite City, I experienced an incident that might best illustrate the magical hold a lost treasure has over us. It was a hot sunny day and I was alone as I walked slowly over the old townsite with a metal detector in my hands. I was aware that a lost bucket of platinum was supposed to be buried somewhere on the old townsite, but that was the farthest thing from my mine as I found nails, gun shells, tobacco tins and even the occasional pull tabs. About two hours into my search, I received a particularly strong signal. Unlike the other objects I had found, the source of this signal was, as it turned out, about six inches below the surface.

I do not recall any special excitement as I began clearing away the earth until the lid of an old iron pot began to appear. It was about eight inches in diameter, and as I began to widen the hole to enable me to remove it, my heart began to pound excitedly while my mind began to race off in all directions. What was below the lid? Was it the lost bucket of platinum, or an almost equally valuable cache of gold and silver coins?

As I frantically dug at the dirt, I glanced nervously about, concerned that someone else might happen by before I could claim my treasure. At last I had removed enough dirt to allow the removal of the lid, which I grabbed by the handle and yanked out in one quick motion. To my amazement, there was nothing below but dirt. There was no treasure, just a rusted iron pot lid. But for a few brief moments I had been exhilarated by the unknown and the anticipation of a discovery. The excitement that gripped me as I dug madly at the dirt has remained with me for over 15 years. God knows what would have happened if the lid had actually covered a pot with some valuable treasure.

It is this sense of adventure, of excitement and of anticipation that, I believe, triggers something within us at the mere mention of lost treasure. There's always the mystery of the unknown, and the remote possibility of discovery. Like most readers of this book, I have always been fascinated by lost, sunken or buried treasure. Fifteen or 20 years ago I was gullable enough to accept most treasure stories on blind faith. I must admit that I found it rather odd to read how, time and time again, after discovering a fabulous mine, the discoverer died on the eve of returning to the site. But I dismissed this thought by convincing myself that, if he had indeed returned, there would in fact be no treasure story, since the mine would be properly staked and brought into operation. After all, the author of the story had written in detail about the lost mine or buried treasure, and had supplied dates, names and places. That information had to come from somewhere, so who was I to question the validity of the events being recounted.

As years passed, however, I came to realize that even the most noted historians sometimes made mistakes. Even worse, I soon learned that if a particularly treasure story had been written up several times, almost always they were only different versions of the first story. When it came to treasure stories, no one, it seems, ever bothered to go to the original sources or do any in-depth investigations of the facts. It was as though the mysteries surrounding lost treasures were best left unsolved; it made for a more fascinating story.

It was during this time that I began to view treasure stories differently. The fascination was still there, but now I viewed the story with skepticism and, instead of the adventure of discovering the treasure, I was challenged by validating the story itself. Like a detective trying to unravel the mystery surrounding a complicated murder case, I found myself investigating the facts of the story in an effort to determine if the people, places and events related had existed. It was a tough assignment, complicated by the enormous span of years since the events were supposed to have taken place. But every time a kernel of information shed new light on the subject, whether it helped confirm or deny the existence of the treasure, it was very gratifying.

The collection of treasure stories in this book are, therefore, unlike any you have read before. Although most of the stories themselves are not new, in the past most authors have merely glamorized the possibility that the treasure existed. I have gone far beyond that, spending a great deal of time and research trying to establish whether or not the treasure exist. Surpisingly, I do not feel that this detracts from the story, since it will always be impossible to be 100 per cent certain whether or not a treasure exists. And, when there is even a one per cent chance, the fertile imagination of the true adventure will run rampant. As long as the slightest possibility remains that a treasure exists, despite the odds, there will be dreamers. And lost treasures, after all, is what dreams are made of.

Garnet Basque,

1
SAN JUAN: RIVER OF GOLD

A lost gold mine, nuggets as "big as a man's fist," treachery, and a massacre are the exciting ingredients of what must be one of B.C.'s greatest and least known treasure tales.

PROBABLY the most appealing feature of this forgotten lode is that, unlike the infamous "Lost Creek Mine," deep in the forbidding mountains of the lower mainland, the unclaimed wealth of the San Juan is reasonable accessible — less than 40 air miles from Victoria. Even were an expedition to produce few nuggets, adventurers would not return "empty-handed," for this ruggedly beautiful region yields some of the best hunting, fishing and camping to be found on Vancouver Island.

To begin our bloody story we must reach back to the time of the first white man to venture among these lonely shores, 200 years ago. For the grim facts we must rely upon local Indian legend, passed down by word-of-mouth from generation to generation. Although some details would appear to conflict with the known record, it must be pointed out that historians, time and again, have found Northwest Indian lore to be remarkably accurate.

ORIGINAL LEGEND

According to the story, about 1777, give or take a few years, a Spanish trading schooner probed the Island's southwestern coast, eventually sighting a large native village on a sandspit created by the Gordon River pouring into the sea. Earlier explorers had found Island Indians eager to trade prime furs for hardware, bric-a-brac and trinkets and, with flood tide, the Spaniards anchored in the harbour, reasoning that a large settlement such as this would yield a profitable haul.

Trade went well the first few days, the friendly Nitinats happily bartering away rich pelts for cheap utensils and bolts of cloth. It was not until two seamen decided to go fishing, in the mouth of

(Opposite page) The San Juan River. This photo was taken near the suspension bridge.

(Left) According to the legend, Nitinat warriors, like this naked bowman, followed the unsuspecting Spaniards up the San Juan where they were quickly massacred.

(Below) The attack and massacre of the Tonquin's *crew off the west coast of Vancouver Island. The following day the ship vanished in an awesome explosion, said to have been touched off by one of her wounded survivors. Scores of Indians were killed or maimed in the explosion. The incident had been precipitated when Captain Thorn, annoyed that Chief Nookamis and the other natives were demanding double what he had offered, snatched a fur from the chief, "rubbed it in his face and dismissed him over the side with no very complimentary application to accelerate his exit."*

the San Juan River, across the bay, that the tragedy began to unfold.

The duo had not been angling for long before they excitedly dropped their lines to fish for something far more interesting. For the observant Spaniards had spotted tiny flecks of yellow in the swirling stream — gold!

Panning the gravel with a plate, they recovered several water-polished nuggets — enough to warrant further investigation, the seamen reasoning that it did not take a geologist to realize that the mother lode must be upstream. Rushing back to their ship, they breathlessly told the others. Within minutes, all but the wives of the captain and mate, who had accompanied the voyage, were gripped by that age-old plague, gold-fever. Furs were forgotten as the men cast lots to see who would remain aboard ship to guard the women. Then, that taken care of, the lucky seven packed their gear and headed up the San Juan to find their fortunes.

They were to find only violent death.

The Spaniards were no sooner out of sight than the Indians began casting hungry eyes at the ship. Just a single man stood between them and more booty than they had ever dreamed of — not to mention two fair ladies as slaves. To these original British Columbians tribal warfare, and all its necessary evils, such as treachery, murder and kidnapping, were a way of life. Paddling out to the ship, several braves clambered aboard with plush furs, pretending to offer them in trade. The lone seaman must have been wary of his customers and kept his musket handy, but he could not watch all of the jabbering, gesturing braves. The second he dropped his guard, a knife arched into his back. Stripping the body, the jubilant warriors threw it over the side, seized the women and looted the ship. That grisly chore done, they torched the vessel, which burned to the water line and sank in a hissing cloud of steam.

Overjoyed by their coup, the tribal chieftain lost no time in dispatching 40 of his finest warriors after the prospectors. It was about 30 miles upriver, on the right bank of the San Juan's left fork, the story goes, that the murderous expedition found its unsuspecting quarry three days later.

Hiding in dense forest and salal lining the river, they waited for dawn, then attacked with terrifying swiftness and efficiency. Seconds later, the deed was done, the Spaniards hacked to death. Few of the ill-fated prospectors knew what had hit them.

Ecstatic at their second success, the warriors decided to celebrate on the spot. It was a fatal error, for divine vengeance struck that afternoon in the form of a torrential downpour. For two days and nights, it rained without pause. Almost instantly, the docile San Juan had become a riot of rampaging brown water and charged over its bank sweeping away trees, boulders. . .anything in its path.

The braves, unable to cross, fled downstream to the forks,

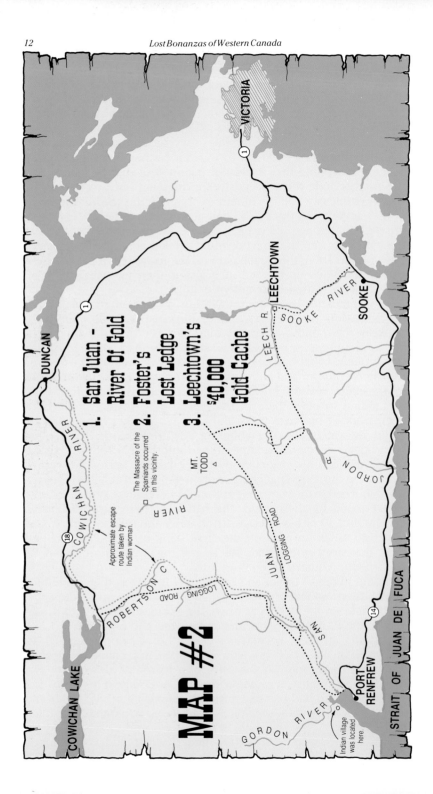

(Above) San Juan beach at the mouth of the San Juan River. The Indian village was located on the far shore.
(Below) "Greeting the Discovery," an original painting by Bill Maximick, depicts friendly natives welcoming Captain Vancouver in 1792.

following the right branch to its source. Here, it pinched off into a series of creeks which would be easier to ford. But their retreat became a rout — then sheer hell.

"Although they had a long journey through a heavily timbered country with frequent patches of dense undergrowth," an early account explains, "they probably would have made it safely without much suffering or loss of life. But while it had been raining in the lower country, it had snowed on the upper reaches of the river. A white, soggy blanket one-and-a-half feet deep lay on the ground, making the travelling slow and tiresome. The days were mild with sharp frosts at night. Unable to build a fire owing to everything being soaked, they suffered terribly from cold and frostbite.

"So the weary days dragged along, the party growing weaker all the time, dying from exposure or falling prey to wolves (which once populated the Island)."

Of the 40 warriors who had stalked the Spaniards up the San Juan, only 19 exhausted braves staggered back to camp, three long weeks later.

The two women, taken as wives by the chief, lived with the tribe for two years until a Spanish man-of-war chanced upon the scene and a squad of armed marines effected their release.

The ship had then sailed away — but not without exacting a heavy toll for the Indian's treachery. The Spaniards left several presents in token reparation for the women and, in so doing, whether by design or accident, doomed the village almost to a soul, as the gifts of bedding harboured a deadly smallpox virus. Weeks later, only four of more than 400 persons survived, the village subsequently being abandoned.

SUMMARY AND CONCLUSION

Verification of this tribal legend may be lying in some musty Spanish archives today. Evidence of Spanish activity along the west coast of Vancouver Island is well documented. The first Spanish vessel to ply the North Pacific was the corvette *Santiago*. She sailed from San Blas, California, on January 25, 1774 and reached sight of the western seaboard of the Queen Charlotte Islands on July 18, the first land spotted since their departure. After trading with the Haidas, the *Santiago* returned to San Blas.

The fact that the natives could be treacherous without provocation is illustrated by the second voyage of the *Santiago*, which sailed north from San Blas accompanied by the little schooner *Sonora* on March 16, 1775. On July 11th the northwest coast was spotted at a latitude given as 48° 20'; from which the Spaniards searched southward in vein for the entrance to the Strait of Juan de Fuca. The Spaniards anchored near Point Grenville and put ashore on July 14: "Bruno Heceta, the Padre, Pierre, the surgeon, Davalos, and Cristoval Revilla, the second pilot, landed with a few sailors and, after erecting a cross, with due ceremony took possession of the country in the name of the Sovereign King of Spain."

So far as is known, these were the first Europeans to set foot on the northwest coast. Meanwhile, the *Sonora* had sent a few men ashore in quest of water in the only boat. "Scarcely had they landed, however, when the Indians to the number of 300 rushed out of the woods and overwhelmed the small Spanish force." The crew of the *Sonora,* unable to get within range of the shore, watched helplessly as the small force was murdered. The Indians then attacked the *Sonora* from their canoes, but were repulsed with the loss of six men. But, had it not been for the timely arrival of the *Santiago,* the *Sonora* would soon have fallen victim also.

Over the years other expeditions followed. The Port of San Juan was named by Manuel Quimper, one of the first Spaniards to visit the area. He arrived in command of the *Princess Real* in 1790. It is interesting to note that two years earlier, on July 17, 1788, the longboat of the *Felice* was furiously attacked and nearly captured by natives in the same area as in our story.

As far as is known, Quimper found the natives (the few left, at least) friendly enough. But there is some support for our legend, J.C. Lawrence recording in his *Brief History of Sooke District:* "The San Juan. . .was well known to the Spaniards in the early days, and evidence of their mining for gold on its banks are frequently found. They harbored their small ships at its mouth from which they had a mule train leading to the headwaters."

History books do not record Quimper having done anything more than his job called for, namely exploration. After the famous territorial dispute with Great Britain, which almost led to war, Spain formally withdrew from the Pacific Northwest in March of 1795, ending all official activity in this region.

So ends chapter one of our story. Chapter two concerns our next discovery of gold in the San Juan and, again, we must thank Indian tradition. Several years after the massacre, a New England trading ship visited the village which had since been established at the mouth of the San Juan. During a pause in business, a few seamen toured the encampment, fascinated by the native way of life. Some giggling children playing on the river bank aroused their curiosity; the naked youngsters were toying with "shiny yellow stones" — gold nuggets.

It was a romantic tale which villagers offered the excited sailors.

Many moons before, they said, a Cowichan war party from the Duncan area had attacked the Nitinats. The marauders had captured much booty and many slaves, including the heroine of this legend who had determined to escape at the first opportunity. But the young squaw's greatest handicap had been navigation, as she had no idea of the route back to her village. Finally there came a day when she overheard the Cowichans talking of her people.

This Paul Grignon painting depicts Indians fishing in more peaceful times.

She learned that the Cowichans had planned in the long-ago to travel overland and destroy the San Juan village by travelling up the Cowichan River to Cowichan Lake, and then take the first river entering the lake from the opposite direction in which the sun travelled during the day.

"This was apparently Robertson Creek," deduced Frank Kelley in the *Colonist* in 1956, "which was to be followed until it left them high in the hills at the head of another stream flowing in the same direction as the sun continued to move by day until they reached the village of the Nitinats on the edge of the big sea water."

Waiting until summer when wild berries were ripe, with some scraps of scrounged food in a tiny basket, which doubled as a fish trap, the courageous girl slipped away. Eventually she struggled out of the rain forest at the San Juan and, hurrying downstream, she was home. After a joyous reunion and rest, she told of her adventures. Then she produced a handful of "pretty stones" which, she said, she had broken from a big yellow rock, high up the San Juan. She had pocketed them as playthings for the village children.

Thus, our second reference to fair-sized nuggets from the San Juan. Fascinating legends, both. But do they have any basis in fact? Undoubtedly, for, as I mentioned, researchers have found native legend to be quite accurate. Possible confirmation of the Spanish massacre came 35 years ago, when a Victoria hunter found a rusty cutlass on the grassy eastern bank of the Sooke River, 15 miles inland from the San Juan. To date, the pitted blade has not been positively identified, although illustrations in reference books would indicate the weapon to be of a type used by Spanish and British seamen during the latter years of the 18th century, the period of our massacre.

Complete clues to this tantalizing lost lode might one day be found in the B.C. Provincial Archives in Victoria.

2

FOSTER'S LOST LEDGE

Port Renfrew residents panned every pond and stream,
roaming all over the San Juan River's lonely upper
reaches in order to discover where Foster
got his gold — but all in vain.

ALTHOUGH local Indians had long known of "pretty yellow stones" in the San Juan River, it was not until 1859 that prospectors began to show keen interest in the area. According to the late George Nicholson, in his *Vancouver Island's West Coast*, "As early as 1860 a handful of men recovered gold from the gravel bars of the (nearby) Gordon (River), but results were discouraging and when news of the rich Leech River strike — which occurred about that time — reached them, they abandoned their claims and hit the trail for that area."

Many others packed up the San Juan but soon moved on, disappointed, after reporting only "small quantities" of the precious metal. And there the matter rested until a mysterious American named Foster made his dramatic debut. When he finally departed for the last time, he left an intriguing legacy: men have been trying to retrace his steps ever since!

ORIGINAL LEGEND

It was about 1885 that Foster appeared in Port San Juan (Port Renfrew) with two companions. The close-mouthed trio had trekked overland from Victoria, picking and panning their way along the many streams. Then, somewhere high up the San Juan River, they made a rich strike. At least, that's what Port Renfrew townspeople surmised; Foster and friends were not saying.

Taking the coastal boat to Victoria, the three apparently went their separate ways. They were forgotten by all but a few local diehards who annually hiked upriver to try their luck, always without success. Then, in 1907, who should reappear but Foster, now known as Old Foster. The aging prospector mumbled something about one of his partners having died in San Francisco, the other having disappeared. Laying in a large stock of supplies at the general store, he called on Chief Peter, "The White Man's Guide," as the sign over his door advertised. Hiring the old Indian, Foster headed upstream in the chief's canoe.

"Ten or 12 miles" later, he waved Peter in to shore. Landing, he shouldered his pack and curtly ordered the guide back to town. More succinctly, he ordered Peter not to so much as look back; Peter was to return in precisely six weeks.

Right on schedule, Peter kept the rendezvous with his strange client, canoeing him downriver where Foster boarded the ship. Foster said not a word about his "hunting trip." Then a year passed, Peter almost forgetting him. But, with the summer, the American was back. Once again they made the mysterious voyage upriver, Peter returning alone, then retrieving his passenger six weeks later. For five summers in succession, Foster made his annual pilgrimage to the San Juan's lonely upper reaches.

By this time, Renfrew was obsessed with its visitor's secret movements. Speculation as to the location of his mine — no one doubted for a second but that he was taking out gold, and lots of it — ran wild. Dozens abandoned their homesteads to hike inland, "panning every little pond where bedrock could be uncovered, picking at cliffs and roaming all parts of the valley in efforts to wrench the mystery man's secret from the forest — but all in vain."

Others tried the more discreet approach of following Foster. But the wily miner soon discovered them, and it was not long before his "silent partners" straggled back to town, bitterly cursing their unwilling quarry. Foster, it seems, played rough — at the first unnatural rustling of a leaf, or the cracking of a twig, he snapped off several uncomfortably accurate rounds with his Winchester.

Even old Chief Peter tried his hand. But he wisely saw Foster onto the ship before his son hurried upstream to the spot where Foster usually landed. Alas, the bush-wise Indians were unsuccessful. Beyond the remains of a few camp fires and a miner's pick, they found nothing. Foster's secret remained intact.

Finally, the more persistent agreed to pool their resources. Out of this decision came a crafty plan — a stroke of genius that was to outsmart itself!

Foster arrived as usual the following summer. This time no attempts were made to follow him. Punctual as always, the prospector boarded the steamer six weeks later. But this time he had a friend. It would seem that even Foster, after a month-and-a-half in the rain forest, welcomed a little company and, after a few drinks at the bar, he and his new companion were hitting it off rather well; enough so that the mellowing miner invited the worthy gentleman to enjoy another bottle in the comfort of his cabin.

The strategy was working beautifully, for it had all been planned that the carefully selected agent should be on the same boat as Foster. It was this man's job to ply him with drink, subtly lead him around to the subject of mining, then let nature — and liquor — take its course.

The jovial spy performed well. Before long, Foster was flashing his gold — not just nuggets, but solid chunks of the prized ore, hacked from a ledge high up the San Juan!

Alas, the best-laid schemes o' mice and men. . . . For there was just one tiny flaw in the plot — the spy's drinking ability. Foster had drunkenly babbled away his secret, all right. But, come the morning, his treacherous companion was suffering a king-size hangover. When his friends eagerly questioned him later, they learned not so much as a clue, their agent being able to remember nothing beyond the size of Foster's gold!

Ten years after Foster's last visit, San Juan pioneer Rev. W.E.H. Ellison recalled his mysterious friend to writer John Hickey:

"I knew Foster well. He was an old miner from Salt Lake City. As I gathered the story from him, he had prospected the valley back in the 70s and 80s with two companions and had made a strike of some sort. For some reason it was not until he was an old man, however, that he decided to come back. Then he returned year after year for quite a long period. I grew to know him quite well as he would stop at my cabin. He must have stayed with me six or seven times at least.

"He always told me," Ellison continued, "that he came back looking for the original find he had made and that he could never locate it. Every year he said that. But Salt Lake City is a long way off and it doesn't seem likely that a man, especially an old man, would come all that distance every year just on speculation. Besides, I noticed that he always slept with his bag under his pillow. I think he had something, all right."

The next paragraph of Reverend Ellison's reminiscence should be of particular interest to present-day treasure hunters:

Foster, he said, "always arrived in July when the water was low in the river. That made me think that whatever he found was in the bed of the stream. He would stay about six weeks and then leave. By that time the river would be rising again. Of course it is possible he really was searching for his original location unsuccessfully. The river changes its course so much. One course gets choked with brush and windfalls and the water then makes off in a different direction. The valley is about two miles wide and I have known the stream to wander half a mile from its former bed. Something like that happens every year. So it is quite possible that changes in the many intervening years prevented him from finding his old strike again.

"It must have been about 1917 that he came for the last time. Then he died — at Salt Lake City. Quite a few have tried to find what he looked for but, so far as I know, without success."

SUMMARY AND CONCLUSION

(Above) A fishing boat in Port Renfrew harbour as photographed from the government wharf.
(Below) San Juan beach, at the mouth of the San Juan River. Port Renfrew is in the background.

The suspension bridge over the San Juan River, August, 1986.

Such is the fascinating legend of Old Foster. A second tale parallels this so closely that it can be but a variation. However, in one aspect, at least, it is far more substantial. The name of this legend's protagonist is Todd, not Foster. Maps of the region show a Mount Todd, elevation 3,176 feet, and Todd's Crevice. Attempts to determine the origination of these names, however, which might shed new light on the mystery, have thus far been unsuccessful. However, *British Columbia Coast Names* list a Tod Creek, on the Saanich Peninsula, while *1001 British Columbia Place Names* mentions a Tod Inlet, in the same vicinity. Both of these references, however, are to honour John Tod. Born in 1793, Tod joined the HBC in 1813, arriving in British Columbia 10 years later. After an illustrious career, Tod retired and settled in Victoria, where he died on August 13, 1882. Is it possible that Todd Mountain and Todd Crevice, spelled with two "d's," were named in his honour as well? It would appear unlikely, but until research can provide more details, one can only speculate.

The whole of southern Vancouver Island is rich in mining lore. Famous Leechtown, as has been mentioned, has been the scene of much excitement over the past century. Even today it yields some of the purest gold to be taken from nature's vast storehouse. However, although thousands have searched this rugged region, most were convinced they had merely scratched the surface. The Mother Lode, they stated emphatically, still awaits some lucky finder.

According to *Methods of Placer Mining:* "In one 35-mile stretch on the west side of the island, from Port Renfrew south to the Sooke River, there are quite a number of gold streams, including the Gordon River, the San Juan, the Sombrio, Loss Creek, the Jordon, the Leech and the Sooke. All of these flow westward and all have their origin in the old 'Leech River Formation,' from which so many of the island's placer streams flow."

The 1893 *Minister of Mines* may have provided an important clue to this lost ledge of gold, if in fact it exists, when it reported: "Gold has been found in nearly all the streams draining into San Juan Harbour. There are some good looking quartz ledges between McDonald and Fleetwood Creeks, which flow into the San Juan river where the Leech River Trail strikes it."

Is it possible, then, that Old Foster, or Todd, stumbled upon his bench of solid gold, not at the headwaters of the San Juan, but somewhere in the vicinity of the headwaters of McDonald or Fleetwood Creek? Since the Leech River, Jordon River, McDonald and Fleetwood creeks all drain from the same area, this could be an invaluable clue.

In recent years the Leech River has even been worked by SCUBA divers. More recent still, a number of one-half ounce and one ounce nuggets and other coarse gold have been found by snipers. No one, however, has yet found a trace of Foster's (Todd's) fabulous gold ledge.

Today, it is a relatively easy drive from Victoria to Port Renfrew. From Port Renfrew, well-maintained logging roads lead into the San Juan River area. It is even possible to reach the Leech River area by the backroads. A word of caution, however. The roads are unmarked, and it would not be difficult to take a wrong turn and drive aimlessly for hours, especially at night.

3

LEECHTOWN'S $40,000 GOLD CACHE

Legend has it that the treasure was buried in the ghost town of Leechtown in a "knee high rubber boot, covered with an inverted frying pan," less than two feet below the surface.

GOLD was first discovered on Leech River in July 1864 by Peter J. Leech. When word of the discovery leaked out, prospectors from near and far swarmed in with expectations of a rich strike. Within a few weeks Leechtown was booming, and some even feared it would "depopulate the city of Victoria." In August the *Sierra Nevada* arrived at Sooke with over 100 gold-hungry California miners. All were headed for the new goldfields at Leech River.

Anxious to promote the goldfield in its back yard, the Victoria papers printed glowing stories of rich strikes and of how large nuggets were easily claimed from the river. The gold dust, of a rich yellow colour, assayed $18.40 to the ounce. High expectations were held for Leechtown, and for a while claims like the Scandinavian and Mountain Rose seemed to live up to them. Reports of wages as high as $22 a day were not uncommon.

Soon the little town on Kennedy Flats was teeming with mining activity. Saloons and dance halls opened up, and the liquor merchants carried on a lucrative trade. By the first winter the population had soared to 5,000, and Leechtown boasted 1,200 miners.

The Leech River gold rush, the strike many believed was richer than the Cariboo, soon began to decline, however, and by late 1865, most of the miners had drifted off to new strikes and new dreams. Those who had expected the Leech River gold rush to equal or surpass the California and Cariboo goldfields were sadly disappointed, and as rapidly as it had boomed, Leechtown died.

Today, trees and salal have completely overrun the old townsite and, thanks to the assistance of vandals, little evidence remains of this once bustling, gold mining community.

The Berks Hotel at Leechtown, 1865.

(Above left) Lieut. Peter Leech, discoverer of gold on the Leech River.
(Above right) This vandalized cairn marks the spot of the Gold Commissioner's cabin. It is constructed of rocks from the collapsed remains of the cabin's chimney. There was once a brass plaque on the cairn explaining its significance. (1977)
(Below) The Government House, Leechtown.

ORIGINAL LEGEND

Most of the versions of the Leechtown treasure would appear to have originated with an article written by James K. Nesbitt in *B.C. Digest.* Mr. Nesbitt's primary source of information was W.T.H. Lubbe, one of Leechtown's last remaining residents.

According to Mr. Lubbe, outlaw "Rattlesnake" Dick Barter and his gang had robbed a Wells, Fargo muletrain in the 1870s, escaping with $40,000 in gold dust. Barter knew that stolen gold dust and nuggets could be easily identified on close examination. An assayer could tell by its quality, roughness or smoothness, not only from what country it came, but also the region, and many times the very river or stream. More than one robber has been trapped by this method, as vividly illustrated by the capture of Sam Rowland (see *Gold From the B.X. Stage*).

Realizing this, Barter devised an ingenious plan by which he could dispose of the stolen gold undetected. He would smuggle the treasure to the distant gold camp of Leechtown and bury it. Then, extracting small quantities from time to time, he would sell it under the pretence of panned, Leech River gold. With the Leech River gold rush then in full swing, he would not draw attention to himself.

Barter pitched a tent somewhere along the banks of the Leech River, buried the gold, then lived it up in the saloons and dance halls. All apparently went smoothly, so the story goes, until the day a United States marshal arrived with a warrant for his arrest. It is not recorded how the marshal knew where to locate Barter, but he was captured and returned to California where he was incarcerated in either Folsam or San Quentin prison. A short time later Barter became seriously ill and it was obvious he would not recover.

Before he died, Barter apparently revealed the location of the missing $40,000 gold cache to the prison warden, who, after Barter's death, left for the Leech River goldfields in the company of two men. It was reported that Barter had admitted burying the gold in "a knee high rubber boot covered with an inverted frying pan, the bottom of which was less than 18" below the surface."

Leading packhorses loaded with food, tools and supplies, the warden and his two companions arrived in Leechtown where they spent a week searching for the hoard. After that time, they simply abandoned their equipment and left. Those who had learned the purpose of their visit were convinced they left the treasure behind also.

In 1915, an old prospector named Captain Martin lay dying in a hospital bed. He had been a prospector at Leechtown during the time Barter was reported to have buried his stolen loot and he claimed to know the location. But his deathbed description of the treasure site was either confused, uncertain, or the senile imagination of an old man, for with his dying breath he revealed the location as being, "150 yards, or feet, or 250 yards or feet, northwest from the northwest corner of the largest building in Leechtown."

There were two large buildings in Leechtown at that time: the Government House and the dance hall. Hopeful searchers have measured the stated steps from both in their quest for the gold — with negative results.

How Captain Martin came to know the treasure site remains a mystery. However, he was known to be a good friend and associate of William Ralph, a professional engineer, who had himself sought out the elusive hoard from time to time.

Ralph, who resided in Victoria over the saloon run by Tolmie & Stewart on Yates Street, kept pretty much to himself as far as the treasure was concerned. But it was his strange custom to go down to the saloon, neither drinking nor speaking, and sit for hours. Ralph was an excellent listener, however, and often picked up pieces of conversation that had been pried loose by the booze. It is assumed he gained knowledge of the treasure in this manner.

According to Lubbe, when Ralph was surveying for the Esquimalt and Nanaimo Railway, he made his headquarters at Goldstream House. This was where the trail started through the woods to Leechtown, and it was here that the warden and his party arrived one morning on their way to Leechtown. It was here, also, that the party regularly picked up their mail. Lubbe surmised that Ralph "heard interesting scraps of conversation" about the buried treasure in the barroom.

Ralph, who was a frequent visitor to the Lubbe household, was convinced the warden's search had been unsuccessful. "Ralph did not believe the warden found the treasure," declared Lubbe, "and I know that Ralph did not get it, because my father, in company with Duncan Stewart was a co-executor of Ralph's will and the affairs of the estate showed no sudden burst of prosperity. Old man Martin did not get it and I know that Paddy Dineen and myself did not get it."

THE ROBBERY

After the death of his parents in Quebec City, Richard H. Barter, along with his brother, sister and her husband, moved to the United States. In 1850 they made the long journey to Oregon where they were enticed by news of the great California gold rush. Everyone was talking about Rattlesnake Bar on the American River, and in the spring of 1851, the brothers joined the rush.

After a year of unrewarding labour, Dick's brother became dejected and returned to Oregon. Dick, however, refused to leave, and because of his dedication and confidence that Rattlesnake Bar would make a comeback, he was given the nickname "Rattlesnake."

"Rattlesnake" Dick first ran afoul of the law in July when the

(Above) The first log house on Leech River, Mountain Rose claim.
(Below) Stores on Kennedy Flat, Leech River.

proprietor of a general store accused him of stealing cattle. The man apparently had a personal grievance against Dick, and, although tried and acquitted, it had put a stigma on his name. Later that year he was in trouble again. When a Mormon reported seeing Dick in the vicinity on the day his mule was stolen, young Dick was arrested and tried. Convicted, Dick was sentenced to two years in state prison. He was still in Folsom when the true culprit was apprehended with the animal.

With his name unjustly tarnished a second time, Barter changed his name to Dick Woods and headed for Shasta County, 200 miles north. Three years later he joined the rush to French Gulch, where he had the misfortune of meeting someone who had known him at Rattlesnake Bar. Identified as Dick Barter, and unjustly branded a two-bit thief, Dick was forced to move on yet again.

After days of brooding, Barter shoved his pistol into the face of a traveller and relieved him of $400. He had made his decision — if he was going to be branded a thief anyway, he might as well enjoy the spoils. So during the summer of 1856 he pursued his new career of road agent with unqualified success.

Eventually Dick decided to form a gang and selected five men from a score of the elite of California's worst. The dreaded band comprised six men: Rattlesnake, the leader; George Skinner, Barter's trusted friend and second lieutenant; George's brother, Cyrus Skinner; a fast drawing young Texan named Bill Carter; a big, husky horse thief known as Adolphe "Big Dolph" Newton; and an Italian named Nicorona Romero.

In his day, Rattlesnake Dick and his band of cutthroats were sought by posses from three California counties: Placer, Eldorado and Amador. For three years they terrorized the countryside until the pressure from the law became too intense. Forced to flee the area, Barter chose Shasta County as his next base of operations.

Once there, Dick wasted little time in plotting his next hold-up. He planned to rob a Wells, Fargo muletrain along a gruelling pack trail that wound its way from Yreka to Shasta. Realizing that the Wells, Fargo mules bore a special brand that could be easily identified, Barter decided to steal replacements. So, while the other five men under George Skinner (a Mexican had been added to the band for this job) set out on foot in search of a robbery site, Barter and Cyrus went off in search of mules.

George Skinner chose as his location a bit of semi-level ground somewhere between Iron Mountain and Sugarloaf Peak, where they concealed themselves in a cluster of jackpine, spruce and cedar, and waited. A small creek running nearby would provide the fresh water they needed.

Throughout the night and all during the next day they took turns watching for the muletrain. When there was no sign of Dick and Cyrus around midday, George sent two men back along the trail to see if they had gotten lost. The men returned that night without having seen any sign of Dick, Cyrus, or the mules.

It was nearly noon of the next day when the heavily laden mules were observed in the distance. Although the four mules were driven by two muleskinners and flanked by four armed guards, the bandits fell upon them so quickly and suddenly, that they surrendered the gold shipment without firing a shot. The mules were then quickly relieved of their burden and stampeded out of sight. After the six men who had accompanied the gold shipment were tied up, George and company sat down to await the arrival of Dick and Cyrus.

That night while the Mexican slept (he was supposed to be on guard) the six men slipped their bonds and headed for Shasta City. When George learned of the escape the following morning, he became angry with his Mexican sentry. An argument ensued and the Mexican foolishly went for his knife. George promptly fired three .44 calibre slugs into the Mexican, killing his instantly.

There still was no sign of Dick and Cyrus, but they could not afford to wait any longer. They were without horses or pack mules, and the escaping guards would soon lead a posse right to them. George quickly reached his decision. They would carry out half of the stolen gold, about 50 pounds per man, and bury the remaining 200 pounds that constituted Rattlesnake's $40,000 share. Rattlesnake would have to return for it later.

While the others were busy breaking camp, George struggled up the mountainside dragging 200 pounds of gold. He was gone for a considerable time, although he could not have dragged such a heavy load very far. When George returned to camp he refused to reveal the hiding place to the others. The four men then divided up the remaining 200 pounds and started out.

Fearing they would eventually be captured on foot, the gang stole horses at the first opportunity. Then, after hiding their stolen gold in a cave near the settlement of Folsom, they decided to celebrate their good fortune at Jack Phillip's "Mountaineer" tavern. Then they made a fatal mistake. Since they still had not heard from Dick or Cyrus, George decided to look for them in Auburn.

About 12 miles outside Auburn, they met up with the posse headed by Wells, Fargo detective, Jack Barkeley. Confronted by the lawmen, Ramero panicked and made a run for the American River which was nearby. He was wounded in the back by one of the posse members, but managed to hide in the underbrush near the river. He was later captured while trying to swim across and returned, with Carter and Newton, who had surrendered, to stand trial. George Skinner was not as fortunate. He made the fatal error of trying to outdraw Barkeley and was instantly killed by a bullet in the forehead. With him died the secret location of the $40,000 buried on Trinity Mountain.

Newton and Romero were sentenced to 10 years each in the

penitentiary. Carter turned State's evidence and was later released after leading officials to the $40,000 that was hidden in the cave.

And what of Dick and Cyrus? They were never implicated in this particular robbery. It seems they had a perfect alibi: during the robbery, and the events that followed, Rattlesnake Dick Barter and Cyrus Skinner were being detained in the Auburn jail! They had been there since the first night, when they had been caught red-handed in the mule corral. Before they could be brought to trial, however, they escaped. Cyrus Skinner was recaptured a few days later and sent to state prison for four years. Rattlesnake Dick put together a new gang and continued his evil ways for another two years. According to *Road Agents and Train Robbers,* the end finally came "in the early evening of July 11, 1859."

At 8:30 a neighbour pounded excitedly on the door of sheriff George Martin. He had just seen Rattlesnake and a companion on the road heading north. Several minutes later Martin, along with deputies Johnson and Crutcher were racing in hot pursuit. In the clear, moonlit night, they soon approached two riders in the distance. As they closed, Johnson ordered the men to pull up and raise they hands. Cornered, the outlaws came up firing. "Dick's bullet severed Johnson's rein and mangled his left hand. His companion's slug struck Martin in the chest and tumbled him from the saddle. Crutcher, not knowing that Martin was dead, dropped down to see what he could do for him."

Up to this point no shots had been fired at the bandits, and it appeared that they would escape untouched in the confusion. "But Crutcher straightened up and fired a shot. Johnson, getting control of his mount, did likewise."

Both men later testified that they had seen Rattlesnake sway in the saddle before spurring his horse down the road.

Although a posse searched all night, they discovered no trace of the outlaws. However, the next morning the passengers of the Iowa Hill stage found a dead man near the Junction House. Close examination revealed he had been shot twice through the chest and once in the head. Deputy sheriff Crutcher later identified the dead man as Rattlesnake Dick. Since Crutcher and Johnson had only fired one shot each, the third wound could not be accounted for. Because Barter's corpse had no money on it, the remains had to be buried at the county's expense.

SUMMARY AND CONCLUSION

It is readily apparent after reading the actual account of the robbery that no treasure exists at Leechtown — not Rattlesnake's $40,000 at any rate. The possibility of such a treasure has more holes in it than Barter's corpse. Granted, Rattlesnake's gang did rob a muletrain of $80,000 of which $40,000 remains unrecovered to this day. But how it came to involve the little gold camp at Leech River is anybody's guess.

The collapsed remains of a more recent building at Leechtown, 1977.

Remember, only one man, George Skinner, knew where Barter's share of the booty was buried. He concealed it somewhere on Trinity Mountain, told no one where, then took the secret of its location to the grave. Since Barter was in jail during the actual robbery, the concealment of the gold by George Skinner and his subsequent death at the hands of Jack Barkeley, there is absolutely no way he would have learned of the burial site.

Another serious flaw in this treasure tale, is the date of Barter's death. If Rattlesnake Dick was dead and buried in July of 1859, it would be very difficult indeed for him to put in an appearance during the Leech River gold rush that began five years later.

The only way the treasure could possibly be buried at Leechtown is: (1) IF, by some fantastic amount of luck, Rattlesnake managed to find Skinner's hiding place after the area was scoured by hundreds of men who failed to find a trace. (2) IF, Barter possessed enough willpower to have $40,000 for a period of eight years without spending it, (3) IF, again through some fantastic luck, he somehow managed to smuggle the gold across the border into Canada — all 200 pounds of it! (4) IF, the authorities were mistaken about the identity of the dead man discovered on the morning of July 12, 1859, and (5) IF, Barter ever visited Leechtown — there is no evidence to suggest that he ever returned to Canada after going to California.

So, if you are hellbent on searching for Rattlesnake Dick Barter's missing $40,000, may I suggest you sink your spade in the ground somewhere along the old trail between Iron Mountain and Sugarloaf Peak in Shasta County, California. You may not find the treasure, but at least you will be in the right country, for the 200 pounds of gold never left California!

4

LEGEND OF THE LOST CREEK MINE

The Lost Creek Mine is the best known and most sought after mine in B.C. history. Yet, the elusive mine remains lost, leaving us with two nagging questions. . . Does it exist? Is it worth $100,000,000?

September 9, 1890 — SHOT DEAD
Louis Bee, a halfbreed, is deliberately shot and killed by an insane Indian named Slumach, at Lillooet Slough. . . .
January 16, 1891 — PAID THE PENALTY
Slumach, the murderer of Louis Bee, pays the penalty of his crime. Old Slumach was hanged in the yard of the provincial gaol this morning at 8 o'clock, for the murder on September 8th last, of Louis Bee, a halfbreed. . . .

☆   ☆   ☆

MORE than three-quarters of a century after, these two related newspaper reports, spaced four months apart, recall one of the most intriguing, bizarre — and, in a sense, unsolved — mysteries from out of British Columbia's past.

More to the point, they recall the Pacific province's greatest tale of lost treasure; one which has been pondered over, searched for, and publicized so many times over the past 96 years that, today it is virtually impossible to distinguish fact from fiction.

The legend of Slumach's "Lost Creek Mine" has reached epic proportions since its unusual "protagonist" went to the gallows, one cold January morning in 1891. I will attempt to give all the facts which have been recorded to date and, hopefully, help modern-day treasure hunters decide for themselves whether or not Slumach's fabled hoard of rich nuggets actually does exist in the forbidding mountains beyond Pitt Lake.

Beginning with the facts, we find that the first time Slumach (also called "Slummock" and "Slumack") gained the attention of the press was on September 8, 1890, when word reached authorities that he had cold-bloodedly murdered half-breed Louis Bee.

"WESTMINSTER, B.C. September 9 — A deliberate murder was committed at Pitt River yesterday by an old Indian named Slumach, who, while fishing with other Indians, picked up a gun and shot Louis Bee, a half breed, through the breast, killing him instantly. After the killing, Slumach reloaded his gun and went into the woods where he now is. The other Indians present were too frightened to detain him. Word was immediately brought to the city, and to-day Mr. Moresby and Capt. Pittendrigh went to the tragedy. Slumach will make a fight before he is captured, but Mr. Moresby is not the sort of man to let possible risk interfere, and will bring him in dead or alive."

Just what did occur at Pitt River (actually the murder took place on the banks of the Alouette River), that September day, will forever remain a mystery.

The day after the slaying, the New Westminster *Daily Columbian* reported that "another startling phase" had developed in the "Slumach-Bee" case when the murderer returned to the scene of the crime (in time-honoured tradition) to drive away the Indians guarding Bee's body. Waving them off with his rifle, he bundled the corpse into a canoe and, paddling out into the river, deposited it in deep water before returning to shore, where he "disappeared again and no trace of him can be found."

This attempt to dispose of the *corpus delecti* did no more than delay Coroner Pittendrigh's investigation, however, that official having the Indians drag for Bee's body, which they recovered the next morning. As he organized an inquest, Pittendrigh reported that there was "intense sorrow among the Indians over the occurrence."

On September 12, it was reported that Slumach was still at large, with Gov. William Moresby (who doubled as a warden of the New Westminster penitentiary and as deputy sheriff) on his trail. Two days after, Slumach rated greater newspaper coverage when it was said that Bee had not been his first victim. By this time, Slumach had succeeded in eluding his pursuers, authorities fearing that "there is no immediate prospect of his capture, unless he is driven by starvation into the haunts of men."

The previous day, Moresby had scouted the shores of Pitt Lake without finding a trace of his elusive quarry, although, just before his arrival, local Indians had spotted Slumach at his cabin. Upon realizing that he was observed, the murderer had plunged into the forest, not to be seen again that day.

When Moresby arrived at the killer's shack, he found a can of gunpowder and a large quantity of provisions, which he destroyed before burning the cabin to the ground so as to prevent Slumach's using it as a shelter, thereby forcing him to take to the woods until approaching winter, or hunger, drove him back to civilization.

Undaunted by not locating his man, Moresby "left for Pitt Lake

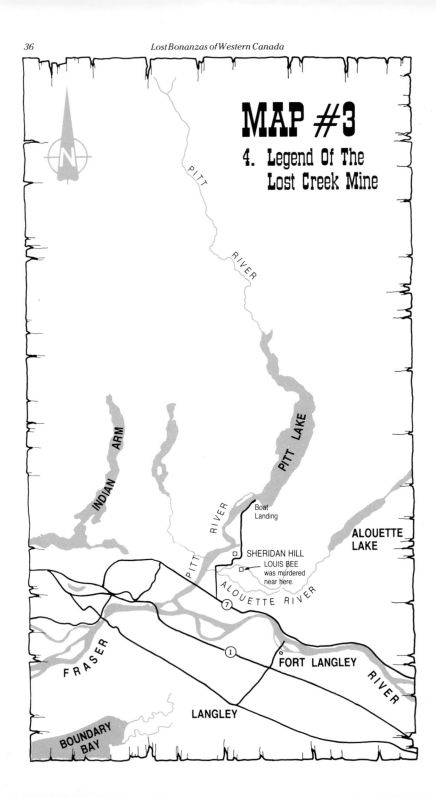

MAP #3

4. Legend Of The Lost Creek Mine

again Friday morning, and may not return to the city for several days. He is determined to bring Slumach to justice and will, if he can, obtain the assistance required. The Indians are all afraid of the murderer, and decline to assist in beating the bush for him, as he is well armed and has lots of ammunition. Slumach is a desperate character, and is credited by the Indians with another murder, committed years ago. Although a few of the murderer's friends say he is insane, dozens of Indians who know him say otherwise, and declare he is only a bloodthirsty old villain."

Whatever his state of mind, there was no denying that Slumach was a formidable foe in the bush, which he knew better than any of his pursuers.

Although Moresby had not seen hide nor hair of the slayer, Constable Anderson had come considerably closer, having spotted him at Pitt Lake and fired four long-distance shots before Slumach vanished once more. One of the greatest problems in bringing him to bay apparently was the fact that his relatives remained loyal and actively assisted his flight, even "act(ing) very ugly" towards Moresby, who, to settle the matter, had them removed to the Coquitlam reserve with promises of "dire punishment" if they returned to their homes at Pitt Lake before Slumach was apprehended.

As days passed without his capture, his list of reputed victims grew, it being reported that, according to "Indians who know him well," he had committed no fewer than five murders during the previous 25 years. His last victim (prior to Bee) had been the original owner of the cabin Moresby had put to the torch. Six years earlier, it was said, he murdered that unnamed Indian without "any apparent cause," and fled into the bush where he hid for a year before daring to return to occupy his victim's shack.

Slumach was, said the *Columbian,* "looked upon by the Indians as a very wonderful person, being able to endure the greatest hardships without apparent inconvenience. As a hunter he is without an equal, and he is adept at making fires in the primitive manner, using two sticks and rubbing the same together until the friction ignites the wood. He is said to be without fear of man or beast and to be possessed of a nature vicious in the extreme."

Slumach's fabled ability to live off the land went unchallenged when he continued to defy Moresby's energetic efforts to bring him in. Again the noted lawman headed up Pitt Lake on the little steamer *Constance,* only to return to town without so much as the glimpse of his prey, although Constable Anderson enjoyed the dubious pleasure of a second long-range glimpse of the outlaw, who, when last seen, was standing on a rocky bluff, armed with his deadly rifle, and wearing nothing but a red shirt and handkerchief tied about his head. This time, he was too far away to exchange shots, and "quietly retreated into the impregnable fastnesses among the stupendous precipices that frown over the lake at the neighbourhood."

Without question, it was the very ruggedness of the terrain that ensured Slumach's freedom; at least, as long as he was able to provide for himself. His hunters were sure that, with winter, he must, for all of his extraordinary stamina and ability, risk capture by leaving the bush.

The same news report indicated that Slumach was armed with a shotgun, rather than a rifle (refuted by the bullet removed from Bee's body), and exhorted officials to make every effort to bring him to justice at the earliest opportunity. Curiously, upon reading between the lines, it seems that groups of sightseers were visiting the scene where Louis Bee died, the *Columbian* warning those so inclined that Slumach, armed and decidedly dangerous, was still lurking in the vicinity, and that "carelessness in this matter may result in a still more lamentable tragedy" than that which has already occurred.

This particular issue of the Royal City newspaper is especially significant in the light of later events, in that it sheds further light, as learned from the Indians, on the state of Slumach's mind (an interesting point when one comes to deciding whether or not he found treasure). He had always, his native acquaintances said, "acted strangely, and at irregular intervals would withdraw himself alone into the forest that border for weeks, reappearing at the end of those periods of aberration looking haggard, and more like a savage beast than a human being. In spite of his lunacy, however, the maniac never displayed any signs of hostility (five alleged murders notwithstanding!), nor gave indications that his freedom was dangerous to human life.

"He is described as a very powerful man and is rather dreaded by his own Indian friends."

One of these very same friends informed the local Indian agent that he had seen Slumach in the bush and that, from the wanted man's looks, "he had not the slightest doubt that he would murder the first man he met."

The same report also throws light upon poor Louis Bee, Slumach's "latest" victim, describing him as having been of remarkable strength and as having had a king-sized thirst. Once, it was learned, the "splendid specimen of the half-breed," crazed by too much liquor, went berserk in town, it requiring six strong men — exercising "dogged perseyervance" — to drag him, kicking and struggling every inch of the way, to a cell. However, but for this failing, Bee was said to have been considered quiet and respectable.

There had been at least one new development in the case, Pitt Lake Indians having overcome their fear of Slumach and joined in the search; a change which a weary Moresby and his men undoubtedly appreciated.

Days, then weeks, passed with Slumach still at large, despite every effort made by the posse which continued to scour the mountains overshadowing Pitt Lake. They could have saved themselves the trouble, for, with the arrival of winter, Moresby's prediction that Slumach must leave the bush came to pass.

Actually, credit for Slumach's surrender should go to Indian Agent P. McTiernan, who persuaded natives living in the area to forget their fear of the killer and to aid the law. In this way, he succeeded in cutting off any chance of Slumach's obtaining food and ammunition. With the first snowfall, Slumach's days in the bush, for all of his experience, were numbered. (In all deference to Slumach, it should be remembered that he was by no means a young man.)

On the historic date of October 24, 1890, the outlaw sent his nephew Peter Pierre to McTiernan with an offer of surrender. The agent hurried to Pitt Lake with two native policemen, where the "desperate fugitive quietly surrendered. He had eaten nothing for several days, and was in a terrible state of emaciation and thoroughly exhausted. His ammunition was all gone and his clothing in rags, and he presented a very wild and weatherworn aspect."

Rushed to jail in New Westminster, Slumach was placed under care of that institution's medical staff. Due to his age, and apparent condition, the staff doctors were unwilling to express an opinion as to his chances of recovery.

But, nine days later, Slumach was alive and well enough to appear in district court before Captain Pittendrigh, coroner and justice of the peace, for a preliminary hearing. After several witnesses were examined, "and a mass of evidence taken down," he was committed for trial at the November assizes.

"The prisoner has greatly improved in health since his surrender," reported the *Columbian,* "and will be strong enough to undergo the tedium of the assize trial this month. Slumach is rather an intelligent looking man of about 60 years of age. His face expressed a great deal of determination, even ferocity. He sat in court listening to the evidence this morning with the utmost apathy.

"A number of Indians occupied seats and took a great deal of interest in the proceedings."

However, a week later, when it was time for Slumach to appear for trial, officials feared that his undermined condition would not permit him to take his place in the dock on schedule. Described as being very weak, the ungrateful felon seemingly was guilty of bad manners in that he failed to "gather strength so rapidly as might be expected, considering the attention and comforts he receives from the medical superintendent and gaol officials." The fact that they were merely preparing him for the gallows, like the

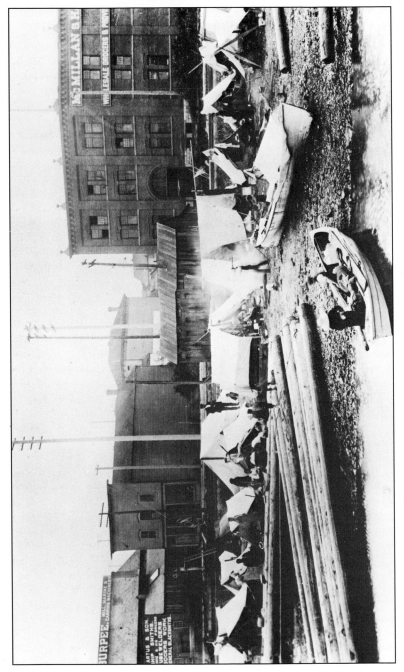

Alexander Street, New Westminster, 1899. After "throwing gold to the four winds," Slumach returned to his mine for more.

fattening of a cow for slaughter, seems to have been lost upon the Royal City reporter.

One who felt that Slumach would not live long in confinement was Indian Agent McTiernan, who voiced it as his opinion that an "Indian sentenced to a long term of imprisonment soon pines away and dies." Others shared this view, convinced that if Slumach proved too weak to stand trial at the November assizes he would not survive in his cell until the spring term.

Two days later, Slumach, despite his frail condition, appeared before the bench on schedule. His counsel, T.C. Anderson, requested an adjournment until the spring assizes, as, said Anderson, two important defence witnesses, an Indian named Moody, and a woman named Florence Reed, could not be produced in time for the current sitting. Moresby quashed this bid for time by assuring Justice Drake that witnesses could be produced by 11 o'clock the next morning. Anderson having to be content with reading into the record the affidavits of Slumach and his daughter, Mary.

The following afternoon, His Lordship and jury listened intently as the evidence of several witnesses to Bee's shooting was given through an interpreter. The result of this testimony was a new, and interesting, portrait of the murder victim, it becoming apparent that Louis Bee had been "in the habit of blustering at, and threatening almost everyone with whom he came in contact. Against Slumach he indulged something like a grudge, and for a long time there was bad blood between them." The result of this animosity, that fatal afternoon, had been a "slight altercation" and Slumach's ending the feud once and for all with a single shot.

The jury was equally short in rendering a verdict of guilty, returning to the courtroom after being out a mere 15 minutes, when Justice Drake sentenced Slumach to hang on January 16.

By Christmas Eve, 1890, the Victoria *Colonist's* New Westminster correspondent reported that Slumach was "getting along nicely and in good spirits," and that the condemned man had expressed his interest in which of the prison staff would hang him, as well as listening with more attention to the priest in attendance.

The remaining weeks fled by, and, early on the morning of January 16, 1891, Slumach prepared to meet his fate. Throughout the previous day, a gang of prisoners had worked to erect the scaffold, which, unlike the usual practice, had to be built from scratch (with the exception of the crossbeam, which had been used to grim purpose before).

By this time Slumach had regained his strength and was eating and sleeping well, maintaining, "under the gloomy circumstances. . .fairly good spirits." During the construction of the scaffold, he had been able to watch the carpenter's every move, and hear the driving of every nail, from a window in the door of his cell. He seemed to follow the project with interest, and betrayed no indication of being affected by the scene.

Daily, Father Morgan and a native interpreter joined him in the death cell for an hour. Although "a bad man in his day, (Slumach) had listened with marked attention to the advice of Father Morgan," and promised to die bravely.

Throughout the death watch, two guards had maintained a vigil outside his cell, it being reported that "a large number of people have called at the jail to see Slumach, but all have been prohibited by an order from the sheriff except his immediate relatives and religious instructors."

In a conversation with Warden Moresby, the same reporter learned that, when Moresby had searched Slumach's cabin, he had found some prison uniforms (half yellow and half dark brown) worn by the penitentiary inmates. Moresby considered it likely that the uniforms belonged to two convicts who had escaped two years before, that Slumach must have aided them in their flight.

As the condemned man's last hours ticked by the final preparations for his exit from this earthly plane were completed by prison officials, admittance of a restricted number of spectators to be determined by special tickets.

Curiously, Slumach's age, at first thought to be about 60, was then believed to be greater — "somewhere in the neighborhood of 80 years!"

According to this source, "When the British military force (Col. Richard Moody's Royal Engineers) came to the Fraser in 1857 (sic), Slumach was then a full grown man. It is said that he has confessed to killing 10 men in his time, but among the older Indians would not be considered very bad. Before the arrival of the missionaries here human life was as cheap an article as there was on the market. . . .

As for rumors that Slumach had confessed to Bee's slaying, the newspaper replied that they were without foundation, that "if he does so (confess) it will be to his religious comforters and not to officials or strangers."

Throughout his final hours, said Moresby, Slumach "betrayed no symptoms of alarm or care at the sight of the scaffold and evidently does not give the subject very much consideration."

Up early, Slumach enjoyed the spiritual ministrations of Father Morgan and two assistants. As he was led to the scaffold he had to be helped, as he showed signs of being very weak. But, under the supervision of Sheriff Armstrong, the grim ceremony proceeded without delay. Moments later, at precisely 8 o'clock, he plunged earthward. Three minutes and 58 seconds later, he was pronounced dead, Armstrong and staff being acknowledged for an execution "excellently conducted, (without) a hitch of any kind." Slumach — murder and mystery man — was dead.

The *Colonist* account differed somewhat from that given by its local contemporary, the Victoria *Times,* stating that Slumach remained cheerful to the end, slept well the night before, and finished a hearty breakfast before walking to the scaffold "without a tremor." Minutes before, Father Morgan had at last succeeded in converting him to Christianity, baptising him but moments before the drop. In his last moments on earth, Slumach had faced the crowd of 50 calmly before the noose and hood were adjusted. He died quickly of a broken neck, his body being cut down and buried within the prison grounds after hanging for 20 minutes.

Upon his being pronounced dead, reported the *Columbian,* the prison's black flag was hoisted and a large crowd outside, including several Indian women said to be relatives, began to disperse.

Whatever the finer points of his execution, Slumach was definitely dead — but not forgotten! For a century later, his memory is alive and well, not only in B.C., but throughout the Pacific Northwest. And this — finally — is where the legend of Slumach's Lost Creek Mine — a legend involving mass murder, nuggets the size of "walnuts" from a $100 million El Dorado, and a deadly curse — begins.

All the information given above is a matter of record. It is at this point that legend overpowers so many of those intrigued by the Slumach story to the point that fact becomes indistinguishable from fiction.

Perhaps, this is a good time to apologize for such a long-winded introduction, before getting down to the nitty-gritty. But, as this is intended as a definitive study of the Lost Creek Mine, I felt it necessary to give the full, fascinating story leading up to Slumach's hanging. For much of the legend concerning his "lost bonanza" hinges upon the murder for which he paid the ultimate penalty in 1891.

In fact, before getting into the grey fringe where imagination seems to have taken control, it is worth recapturing Louis Bee's shooting, that September afternoon of almost a century ago. We have learned that Slumach was, to put it mildly, considered a dangerous customer by those who knew him best. We also have learned that Bee was a two-fisted, hard-drinking bully and that there long had been a grudge between them. These are important clues, as, over the past three-quarters of a century, more than one intelligent treasure hunter has attempted to build a case for Slumach's treasure upon his shooting of the half-breed.

According to the initial *Columbian* report, Bee and several Indian companions were fishing for trout in Lillooet Slough (Alouette River), two-and-a-half miles above Pitt River bridge, when Slumach, who had been hunting, stepped from the bush with a double-barrelled shotgun. At his approach, Bee "sauntered up to (him) and asked him in a casual way what he was shooting around there.

(Above left) B.C. Prov. Police Const. Grainger, who, according to the writer who invented him, solved the case of the disappearing wives.
(Above right) Veteran prospector R.A. "Volcanic" Brown who cut off his toes with a pocketknife. . .and fell victim to Slumack's curse.
(Below) The Provincial Goal, New Westminster, where Slumach was hanged.

Without a moment's warning, or any preliminary sign of anger, Slumach instantly leveled his gun at Bee and fired."

A split second before he squeezed the trigger, Bee, upon realizing his intention, raised his hands and begged him not to shoot, Slumach being so close to him that the entire charge entered Bee's body just under his right armpit. Bee died instantly, falling to the ground without so much as a groan, and the manhunt was on.

Subsequent investigation revealed that there had been bad feelings between the two for some time. Thus, a second version of that fatal encounter on the banks of Lillooet Slough sounds considerably more probable. This account, which appears in *Slumach's Gold: In Search of a Legend,* was related by Mrs. Amanda Charnley, daughter of Peter Pierre, Slumach's nephew. Peter Pierre had apparently spent the last few weeks of Slumach's life visiting with him in prison, and it was at that time that Slumach discussed the incident.

Slumach claimed that he was canoeing up to his cabin when he spotted a deer. Mrs. Charnley picks up the story: "He shot the animal from his canoe and then pulled into the beach to look for the wounded animal. After a lengthy and futile search he was returning to his canoe when he saw two Indians in a canoe out on the water. One was Louis Boulier a half French half Kanaka, often called Bee for short, and the other was Charlie Seymour, an Indian from Harrison Mills. Slumach told Peter that Boulier held a grudge against him and stepping ashore came at him wielding an axe and shouting, 'I'm going to chop your damn head off.' Slumach said he raised his shotgun out of sheer fright and fired point blank at Boulier, killing him instantly. Seymour, the only witness, disappeared into the bush. Slumach placed Boulier's body in the victim's own canoe and set it in midstream to drift down to the fishing party. Slumach did not accompany the body because he feared Boulier's friends might mob him. He then got into his own canoe and paddled upstream to his cabin."

We have belaboured the events leading up to Bee's murder so that they will be firm in the reader's mind as we get into the story, for, to this point, there has not been one whisper of a lost gold mine.

ORIGINAL LEGEND

Perhaps the best way to begin is to take one of the hundreds of newspaper and magazine articles which have appeared over the years as an illustration. The example we have chosen was published in the B.C. Provincial Police magazine, *The Shoulder Strap,* in 1942. Titled, "The Bluebeard of Lost Creek Mine," and written by W.W. Bride it states:

"...The existence of the bonanza of the Pitt Lake Mountains district was first revealed some 40 years ago when an Indian from that district appeared in New Westminster who was apparently pretty stakey, since the tales of his wild spending sprees are told with relish by old-timers of the city. Slummoch (sic) was a slim, wiry young Indian, possessing to an unnatural degree the usual Indian taciturnity. Try as they might, neither his fellow tribesmen nor the friendly whites could find the slightest inkling as to the source of his new-found wealth. In spite of the vigilance of his friends he slipped away when his one man Potlach was over. Twice again the town was livened up by the visit of Slummoch. The third gala occasion seemed to pall a little on the red man. Despite his boasts he seemed worried.

"Even as he flung his gold to the four winds and had his moments of importance, the police were engaged in a gruesome task on the banks of the river a few miles north. They were searching the battered body of a young Indian squaw that had been fished from the river. On her person they found several good sized nuggets. She was of Slummoch's tribe. Questioned about her, the young Indian admitted that she had helped him on his last trip to the mountains but had been washed off the raft they made to descend the Pitt River. Although suspicion was rife as to how many others he had helped to disappear, there was not sufficient proof to convict him.

"Some years later, Slummoch again appeared in town and boasted of his wealth and his find in the hills. When pressed as to the location he still refused to tell. . . .

"As before, even as he indulged in his fling, another body was picked out of the river. Although highly suspicious, the police had not sufficient proof for an arrest. Many wondered how many others had gone the same way as the young squaw, since it was certain that no Indian of Slummoch's standing would enter the woods without a squaw to cook and pack for him. . . ."

We'll paraphrase the rest, although the holes in the story are already glaringly apparent.

When next "Slummoch" stalked the streets of the Royal City, this version continues, he was again rich and leading an entourage of four lovely young native women "as he strutted down the main street" on his final fling. But, as before, in almost monotonous routine, police were busy hauling the body of another young woman from the Fraser. This time, however, there was a difference: protruding from her back was a knife positively identified as belonging to Slumach (the accepted spelling of his name).

Arrested and charged with the slaying, Slumach bragged of having killed eight other women whom he had talked into packing for him in the bush by promises of a share of his golden bonanza. Upon their approaching civilization, he had silenced them so as to keep his secret intact. Duly convicted and sentenced to hang, "the clang of the gallows took the secret to eternity."

So much for the legend, other versions of which are more explicit in that they name the bluebeard's pretty victims (one enterprising writer even produced photographs of same which have been published time and again since in Canada and the United States). As we have taken pains to show, Slumach was indeed hanged — but for the murder of Louis Bee, not for that of a woman.

This brings us to the second part of the legend, and, to again quote the *Shoulder Strap* article: "The furore caused by the facts brought out at Slummoch's trial as to the location of his killings was to bring tangible evidence of his valley of gold. This was not to be won easily. More than one hardy prospector bitten with the gold-bug started out in the spring to face the wilds and struggled back months later a beaten and broken man. Fierce mountain torrents, treacherous ice crevasses, starvation and sickness plagued the boldest and accounted for many who never returned. The Pitt River Mountains were reluctant to reveal their secret to the grasping hands of the whites."

There is no denying that the Pitt River Mountains are a deathtrap to the inexperienced. Blizzards, fog and subzero temperatures posing a lethal threat to all who enter this forbidding wilderness, which has been described by those who know it as equal to the worst terrain on the North American continent.

But, according to our legend, there have been those who successfully defied the Pitt River country in search of Slumach's hoard. About 1930, the story continues, a party of Seattle financiers and mining men arrived in New Westminster and proceeded to interview every old-timer and prospector they could find, to learn every fact obtainable about Slumach, his lost mine and the deadly country in which it was situated.

Armed with a letter and map drawn by a prospector named Jackson, they said that he had found "gold beyond his wildest dreams," somewhere to the northwest of Pitt Lake, heading back to civilization with a packsack filled with the yellow metal. But, when Jackson finally staggered out of the bush, he was a beaten, broken hulk of the man he had been, his health ruined by the ordeal.

Jackson did make it back to San Francisco, where, told that he was dying, he wrote all in a letter to a friend in Seattle. Enclosing a crude map of the country, he urged his friend to try his luck beyond Pitt Lake. This man preferred his gold in the hand, rather than in the bush, and sold the map and letter for $1,000. "It passed through many hands in the succeeding years," our storyteller goes on to say, "and was scanned as eagerly as any Captain Kidd ever drew. Years later the bedraggled letter and the smudged map appeared in the hands of the adventurers in New Westminster. Determined to trace the lode down, the party set out for the land beyond Pitt River. They did not find the mine. But they found evidence that Jackson had been there and that he had found gold. Near the head of Pitt Lake they camped. Into the camp came an Indian and a very ancient squaw. It was she who had seen and helped Jackson on his trip out. He had stayed with the party two days.

"Discouraged, the party returned. The towering peaks still hold their secret, guarded by everlasting snow and howling blizzards."

There are numerous minor variations to the story, many being told in greater detail, although the main body of the legend is the same each and every time. If nothing else, several versions show considerable ingenuity and definitely are worth their weight in gold as far as their entertainment value is concerned!

Other writers have linked the mysterious Jackson to Slumach's son. According to this line of thought, before he was executed, Slumach told his son the location of his mine, warning him, "only to go there when times are bad."

But, "scarcely had the executioner cut the old man down from the scaffold, when his whisky-loving son headed for the mountains of Pitt Lake, to lug out "thousands of dollars worth of precious metal" which he exchanged for firewater. Then, for reasons unstated, the younger Slumach took an unnamed half-breed as a partner, the two heading back into the mountains for more gold. Only the half-breed returned, suspected of having severed the relationship with his rifle, with the result that Slumach Jr. became the first of 21 persons (as of this 1952 account) said to have perished in search of the Lost Creek Mine.

However, when the half-breed returned to the "hideous creek. . .lined with gold," he was not alone, having been followed by an American prospector. When next the half-breed visited the lode, he was again followed, by the first miner and a friend, "a veteran Alaskan prospector" named John Jackson. Once at the gold-producing creek, the Americans assumed ownership by shooting their unwitting guide.

"The murderers each toted out a reputed $20,000 from the mine. But only Jackson reached New Westminster. The country swallowed up the other prospector."

It was then that the dying Jackson drew up two maps (according to this version) showing the minesite, giving one to a nurse who had attended him during his final illness, the other going to a Seattle friend named Shotwell. Both parties are said to have sold the maps for $500 each.

Other accounts date Jackson's torturous trek to civilization as 1901 and 1903 respectively, and state that he deposited $8,700 (or $870, or $10,000) in a branch of the Bank of British North America upon his return to San Francisco. Unfortunately for those who claim to have obtained the original letter and map he sent to Shotwell, ". . .some of the letter was illegible, and the map had been drawn from memory, after he got back, and was hard to understand." (At last report, at least two purported copies of Jackson's map were known to exist in Vancouver.)

Whatever the case, the search for Slumach's gold was on, and continues to this day. There is no denying that men have died in their attempts to solve the mystery of the Pitt Lake Mountains (although nowhere as near as many as is popularly estimated).

One of the most fascinating characters to succumb to the legend (and to Slumach's curse, if one believes in Indian legend) was R.A. "Volcanic" Brown, a veteran prospector best known for his Kootenay mining activities. Brown was first linked to the search for Slumach's treasure when, "one night, many years ago," he landed on the doorstep of a Kootenay hunting cabin. Tired and cold, he had accepted the invitation of the cabin's occupants, four Nelson businessmen, to a hot dinner. Then, tongue loosened by liberal quaffs of rum, he told his intrigued hosts of the time he had nursed an Indian woman who turned out to be Slumach's granddaughter. As a reward, the grateful woman had given him the location of Lost Creek.

Thus it was that, year after year, the aging prospector ventured to the headwaters of Pitt River. Although he never said another word as to his activities, and never filed a claim, he always returned to civilization with gold. Despite his advancing years, Volcanic Brown survived the wilds time and time again. Once, caught in a blizzard, several toes became frozen. When gangrene set in Volcanic cut off the ailing members with his pocketknife!

Each year, about mid-September, Brown appeared at the government hatchery situated at the head of Pitt Lake on his return from the mountains. However, in September, 1930, the old prospector failed to show on schedule. When weeks passed, and the season advanced, word that he was overdue was relayed to police, and a search party was organized. Composed of provincial police constable Eugene Murphy, game warden George Stevenson, and brothers Roy and Bill McMaster (trappers who knew Brown), the expedition set out.

A quarter of a century afterward, the late George Stevenson told former deputy commissioner of provincial police Cecil Clark that the search for Volcanic Brown "was the toughest he ever undertook." In 27 horrifying days, Stevenson lost 13 pounds, hiking through sub-arctic blizzards over glaciers that would have killed any but the toughest, most experienced men. When Constable Murphy was injured, Bill McMaster escorted him out, leaving Stevenson and Roy McMaster alone in a frozen world beyond Pitt Lake.

Hiking up to the headwaters of Seven Mile Creek the pair crossed the divide to the mile-and-a-half wide Homestead Glacier, then pushed on to Porcupine Valley and the timberline, before crossing Stave Glacier's seven miles of hummocky ice and snow. Throughout their climb, the two men were attacked by wind-driven snow which cut visibility to zero and forced them to take shelter for five full

days. Once, while crossing Homestead Glacier, they succeeded only in covering 1,200 feet in an entire day!

Somehow they battled their way onward and, finally, at the edge of Stave Glacier, squabbling whisky jacks caught their attention. Upon investigating, they found the remains of Brown's camp under the snow. Of Volcanic Brown himself there was not a trace beyond his few effects: a collapsed pup tent, his single-barrelled shotgun, cooking utensils, a notebook (containing a few scribbled herbal remedies) — and a jar containing 11 ounces of coarse gold which had been hammered from a vein. To this day, no clue as to Brown's fate has been found, it being believed that he perished of starvation, exposure or a fall.

Twenty-five years after the memorable ordeal, Stevenson told Clark that he had had offers of "substantial financial backing" to lead others to Volcanic Brown's last campsite, but had declined. Now both he and Roy McMaster are dead, and Brown's solution to Slumach's secret — if, in fact, his claim had any connection with the murderer — remains another tantalizing mystery.

And so it goes!

In more recent years, others have tried their luck in the deadly Pitt Lake Mountains.

As recently as 1947, a "chubby" Vancouver sign painter named Cyril Walters claimed to have a copy of the letter Jackson gave to Shotwell, which he had obtained in 1922. Walters' copy of the legendary document, he said, indicated nuggets the size of walnuts were "in a place less than 20 miles from the head of the Pitt River, where a stream flows down a canyon and disappears from sight. The canyon is guarded by three peaks which stand as sentinels. I found the peaks and canyon, and followed it to another canyon which fits the description. But I couldn't get down because of ice and snow."

As of September, 1947, Walters had followed Jackson's clues no fewer than 25 summers, and, at last report, planned to make yet another trek into the mountains.

Five years later, headlines in the Vancouver *Province* reported that the legend of Slumach's Lost Creek Mine had been disproved, once and for all. According to J. Stewart Smith, superintendent of securities, a company called the Slumach Lost Creek Mine Ltd. had completed a thorough survey of the area in which the mine was supposed to be located, and found no sign of commercial ore. With this, the company went into liquidation and, for Smith's money at least, "the fantastic story that has lured a number of men to their death has been finally killed."

Unfortunately, few agreed with him, with the result that, in

The entrance of Pitt Lake from the boat launching site. Do the rugged mountains in the distance conceal a valuable mine?

September 1959, three amateur prospectors hiked out of the hills speaking of Slumach's curse. Aldergrove farmers Dan Gray, Alf Newman and Bob Blakey said their search had been thwarted by sudden fogs, mountainslides, lightning storms and rain which had poured for 10 days without stopping.

"There must be something in the curse," said Blakey, "because we didn't find any gold. We weren't exactly frightened, but it certainly made us think."

Two years after, Royal City newspaper editor Elmer McLellan made his own headlines in the *Columbian* with his claim to having found Slumach's mine within a 30-minute drive of downtown New Westminster! By this time, the reputed death toll of those who had perished in their search for Slumach's hoard had risen to 23, inflation having increased the value of his gold hoard to $100,000,000.

McLellan, who did considerable research into the legend, had been told of the site by carpenter-fisherman and former trapper-prospector Wally Lund, of Haney, who "claimed he had a dream which revealed the location to him."

The site indicated by the multi-talented Lund was Sheridan Hill, near Alouette River — and 15 miles from the mountain vault beyond Pitt Lake. One of the reasons that McLellan felt that Lund might be on to something was the fact that Louis Bee had been shot within two miles of the 30-foot deep cavern. According to the newsman's research, Slumach had "hinted that his mine was in the Pitt Lake area, but he told about a creek coming through a hole in a cliff. The cavern at Sheridan Hill apparently at one time had a stream running through it.

McLellan based his theory that Sheridan Hill held the secret of Slumach's long lost mine on the fact that Bee had been killed nearby. As eyewitnesses to the killing testified that Slumach had shot Bee without provocation, McLellan thought it likely that the Indian had had another reason for pulling the trigger and "in so doing commit himself to the life of a fugitive in the weeks that followed, and bring about the physical wreckage that finally surrendered to the law."

In short, McLellan thought it highly probable that Slumach had considered Bee a threat to the sanctity of his mine, just two miles distant: "Was Bee's expedition one for trout, or was he fishing for something more exciting? Was he so near to Slumach's secret, that murder was the only way left to Slumach to protect his find?

"That would have been motive enough."

Also reinforcing his theory was a legend to the effect that Slumach usually returned to town from his mine within 48 hours. Sheridan Hill lies well within this time limit, whereas the mountains beyond Pitt Lake certainly do not.

McLellan staked a claim to 750,000 square feet of ground covering

Sheridan Hill, reputed site of Slumach's lost mine.

the mystery tunnel and took rock samples for assaying. As for old Slumach and his penchant for murdering women he explained: "The old Indian had chosen women for his task as they were nice and light and more easily murdered. For once having seen such a rich cache no one could be expected to keep the secret; no one except the owner."

Alas, for McLellan and Lund, Sheridan Hill proved to be a dud, assay reports denying the presence of gold.

Queried seven months later as to what new developments, if any, had occurred in the case, editor McLellan replied that some local prospectors had poked about the cavern, only to be discouraged by loose rock at the 30-foot level.

The fortune seekers may have been lucky they quit when they did, he said, as it was subsequently learned that they could have been standing upon a rock bridge over a "bottomless pit," the shaft having once been measured to be as deep as 250 feet — when the first explorers ran out of rope. The bridge of rubble apparently had been formed when efforts were made to blast the shaft open. (A local prospector familiar with the site said that it had been an old molybdenum claim.)

McLellan had also learned that Sheridan Hill once had been used by members of the Salish Indians (Slumach's tribesmen) "as a ritualistic centre." The city editor thought it probable that Slumach used the cavern merely as a cache for his gold, knowing that his tribesmen would not trespass.

Spring of 1963 saw yet another search for the Lost Creek Mine end in dismal failure when three Richmond teenagers returned home after encountering cougars, bats and bears. The three, aged 14, 15 and 16, had sneaked away in an 18-foot skiff, powering up Pitt River until they ran low on food, became discouraged and headed back. Their safe arrival ended an intensive search by police, game wardens and fishermen in Georgia Strait.

Early in 1964, the lost mine claimed another victim when 49-year old Bremerton, Washington resident, Lewis Earl Hagbo collapsed and died of a heart attack while prospecting in the area, 30 miles east of Vancouver. His brother-in-law, Frank Mattson, of Bainbridge Island, Washington, had hiked six miles through mountainous country to report his in-law's death, an eight-man RCMP party carrying out the body.

Four years after, 71-year-old prospector Bernard Rover won a 12-day battle against the mountains beyond Pitt Lake by hiking across a glacier and through 10 miles of wilderness after suffering a stroke in his isolated cabin. Amazingly, Rover was reported to be in fairly good condition in hospital after being found by two amateur prospectors, who had spotted his abandoned camp fires.

"We found the old man under a tarp with his legs blown up like balloons," Mike Chizh of Surrey reported. "He was pretty much out of his mind but after we got some food and tea into him he told us he had been prospecting at Thomas Lake for the past month. He said he had suffered a stroke five days (before) in his camp and had set out for help. He couldn't remember anything else.

"He was down to a few hardtack biscuits and a can of sandwich spread. He said he wouldn't have lasted another day without help."

Flown out by helicopter, Rover was rushed to hospital and recovery. As for Chizh, and his partner, Vancouverite Bob Millburn, "We didn't get any prospecting in for ourselves but finding him was much better than finding gold."

Gold, there may very well be in the mountains beyond Pitt Lake. But its link with wily old Slumach is slim. Nowhere in the complete records concerning his shooting of Louis Bee and hanging is there a mention of his ever having amazed the citizens of New Westminster with nuggets the size of walnuts, or that the rumoured notches on his rifle butt included women victims. For that matter, whether or not he was guilty of other crimes remains a matter of pure conjecture, as he was tried only with having shot Bee.

But the legends — particularly those told by Indians of the lower B.C. mainland — live on. If anything, they seem to grow wilder with each passing year. According to native lore, Slumach told only his son of the mine's location with the strict warning that he was to avail himself of its wealth only when absolutely necessary — "go there only when times are bad." It was the son's violation of his vow, said the late Chief August Jack Khahtsahlano, that initiated the 96-year chain of tragedy. Upon rushing to the mine immediately upon his father's hanging, the young Slumach loaded up with gold and hastened back to town, there to find that his newly acquired wealth would buy all but that which he desired most; whisky. Thus his partnership with a half-breed dental assistant, who agreed to keep his whistle wet in return for a 50% interest in the mine. (A totally preposterous idea when one considers that bootlegging to Indians was so common in that age as to be — almost — respectable.)

Whatever, said Chief Khahtsahlano, the two headed into the hills, the half-breed returning "laden with gold" — and alone.

When he reported to work, his annoyed employer fired him for being absent without leave, the half-breed smirking that he did not have to work any more, that he was rich. Intrigued, the dentist questioned him, his former employee proving his claim by flashing a pocketful of nuggets. When the dentist persuaded him that it was dangerous to carry such a large sum of gold, the gullible half-breed handed him the poke for safekeeping with the promise that there was lots more where it came from.

Here, even the Indian version varies, one account saying that the half-breed "journeyed into the rugged Pitt Mountain(s) each August and returned with more gold. Then the curse of Old Slumach caught him. He was seen no more."

A second variation is to the effect that his disappearance was not by curse or by accident. It seems that the dentist told a former school chum, then a prospector, of the half-breed's secret mine. As it was August, and the half-breed was at his claim, the American miner wasted no time in paddling up the Pitt River, to find the other's canoe hidden in the brush. He waited for the half-breed and followed him back to town. The next summer, when the half-breed returned once more to Slumach's gold-lined creek, the American was right on his heels until he lost his trail, high in the hills.

This, according to Chief Khahtsahlano, was where John Jackson entered the picture, in 1903, when he was recruited by the first prospector to help him trail the half-breed. This time they were successful, and upon following him to Lost Creek — "ankle deep in gold" — they shot him and buried his body, an axe, a mining hammer and a pan of nuggets under a "tent" rock, which they inscribed with a cross on one side.

The two, Jackson and his anonymous friend, began hiking out with their packs weighted down with nuggets, estimates of their precious cargoes ranging as high as $20,000 apiece. Only Jackson made it to civilization, his partner joining the Lost Creek Mine's

The Alouette River looking toward Pitt River. It was near here that Louis Bee was shot and killed by Slumach.

roll of victims. Jackson then proceeded to his San Francisco home, to deposit his treasure in the bank and to be informed that the nightmare hike out of the wilds had ruined him. Then, in his final hours, he is supposed to have drawn two maps showing the lost creek, one for his faithful nurse, the other for his old friend Shotwell in Seattle.

According to another source, the late William Pierre (reputedly the oldest member of the Squamish band at the time of his death) was "one of an Indian family who had seen (the Lost Creek Mine's) discoverer, a murderer named Slumach, make bullets of gold." Needless to say, there is no confirmation of this outrageous claim.

A final anecdote told by the Indians claims that, when Slumach was waiting for his final walk in New Westminster jail, one of his wives rushed into town "with a canoe-load of nuggets" with which she hoped to buy his freedom.

SUMMARY AND CONCLUSION

And so it goes — on and on and on. Yet the cold, hard facts remain. Of the records covering Slumach's arrest for Bee's murder, his trial and execution, there is not a single, solitary syllable linking him with murdered wives or a fabulously rich gold mine. Not one.

In fact it was a full 15 years after he went to the gallows that he was first linked in print, with the so-called Lost Creek Mine (and occasionally, Bluebeard). How it became accepted as fact that he was a Bluebeard was hard to say, the reports by fellow tribesmen that he had murdered as many as 10 persons during his career never have been substantiated. As far as the law was concerned, he was guilty only of shooting Louis Bee, and duly hanged. Period.

In an age when the cry of "Gold!" could — and did — change the course of provincial history, there simply is no way that Slumach's fabled trips to town, pockets bulging with nuggets the size of walnuts, would not have touched off a stampede which would have been recorded, in full, breathless, detail by the local press.

When all is said and done, there is but one tantalizing clue in the coverage of his arrest and trial which makes one wonder: That is the *Columbian* column which quotes Slumach's acquaintances as saying that he had always "acted strangely, and at irregular intervals would withdraw himself alone into the forests that border for weeks, reappearing at the end of those periods of aberration looking haggard and more like a savage beast then a human being. . . ."

Was it this quirk which sparked legends of his slipping off into the mountains to visit a rich mine?

As for having murdered several girl friends, or wives, there just is no proof. British Columbia enjoyed one of the finest police forces on the continent, 96 years ago; one whose record precludes any possibility of Slumach having dumped one woman after another into the river without attracting official notice.

Originally, the murdered "wives" were of Slumach's tribe; but with time, and telling, they have become white: Susan Jesner, Molly Tynan, Mary Warne, and Tillie Malcolm. It remained for an enterprising Vancouver writer, working for a now-defunct eastern magazine, to produce not only photographs of the luckless ladies, but also of two provincial policemen involved in the case (neither of whom ever existed), and — tra-la! — one of Slumach himself. The ladies hairstyles and hats, according to retired deputy commissioner Clark, date them as being about 1912-14. As for Slumach (born before the camera was invented!), he is shown as a cigarette smoking scowling man, complete with peak cap, in his 20's. It goes without saying that, at the time of his hanging he was at least 60 years old.

All of which would seem to conclusively dampen the legend of Slumach and his gold mine (although, God knows, I hate to kill a good story!). But this is not to say that the Lost Creek Mine does not exist, although again, concrete evidence is pretty pale.

One of the copies known to exist of Jackson's letter to Shotwell is a fascinating document and, admittedly, has the ring of truth. In it, Jackson told how he had been prospecting for more than two months, when, due to the terrain which precluded his carrying a heavy pack, he found himself running short of provisions. Yet he had pushed on, relying on his rifle for food, and panning every stream he came to. Some showed signs of colour, but not enough to warrant more than preliminary inspection, and growing disheartened, he had resolved to turn back the next day.

That very afternoon, upon topping a steep ridge, he found himself looking down into a little creek which disappeared into the rock. Upon climbing down to the water, his experienced eye quickly noticed a change in the geological structure, and dipping his pan into the white water, he was overjoyed to find rich colour the very first time — "color such as he had never seen before — and he knew his long search was ended."

Following the stream bed, he came to bare bedrock, to find the quartz gleaming with giant nuggets. Loading as much gold as he could carry, Jackson buried more under a nearby rock which was shaped like a tent, upon which he placed an unspecified mark. Then he began the hike out, reaching Pitt Lake in three days, where he first felt ill. By the time he reached San Francisco, he was rapidly failing, and, having no relatives, wrote to old friend Shotwell.

Perhaps the most significant fact about this letter is that Jackson apologized to Shotwell for being unable to give him explicit instructions as to the golden creek's location. All that he could do was to exhort his friend to make an attempt to find it, no matter how long it took.

Did Jackson find a disappearing creek, high in the mountains beyond Pitt Lake, that was yellow with nuggets and dust? (For that matter, did Volcanic Brown?) Interestingly enough, geologists today are convinced that this immediate region is not gold bearing. But, if such a creek does exist, it would seem that, in all justice, it should be called the Lost Jackson Mine!

However, if we accept for one moment that Slumach did find gold, is there a possibility that he obtained it by other means? As one writer has speculated: ". . .That was the time of gold in the Bridge River country, when miners coming and going actually did have pokes with handfuls of gold. Many of them came overland to the head of Pitt Lake where Slumach lay by the trail, his rifle at the ready to dispatch the unwary so that Slumach in a day or two could flash raw gold in the dives of New Westminster.

"Many are the skeletons resting under the leaves in the upper Pitt River country, skeletons of miners never missed in the hurly-burly of a boom era when communications were crude or non-existent and the disappearance of a miner now and then was never a cause for comment."

More recently, another fascinating theory had developed. There are some who believe that the famous Bralorne and Pioneer mines at Bridge River actually were founded on the site of Slumach's "lost creek." Although situated to the northwest of his accepted haunts of Pitt Lake, this country was well within the scope of his travels (had he been so inclined). This line of thought also includes two other Indian characters, Mesachie Sam and Hunter Jack. Some believe his ill-gotten treasure is buried at the foot of Sumas Mountain. Could the names of Mesachie Sam and Slumach have become intertwined over the years?

Hunter Jack, feared by travellers in the Bridge River country as a dangerous rascal, is supposed to have visited New Westminster on several occasions, to celebrate with "a pile of gold." When broke, he would head back into the hills, until the next time he made the rounds of the Royal City saloons with pockets bulging. Lillooet old-timers believe that Jack found his gold where the Bralorne and Pioneer mines were later established, and that he cached several hoards in the area.

But we could go on indefinitely — as the legends of "Bluebeard" Slumach and his lost creek undoubtedly will. In recent years the story even graduated to book form, thus assuring that the memory of the Indian murderer and mystic will continue to tantalize future generations. More recently, the Vancouver *Province* and CKVU Television mounted a combined search for the elusive mine.

For their benefit, perhaps we should refer to Indian legend once more, and conclude Chief Khahtsahlano's assertion that the mine will never be found by a white man. Years before, an ancient tribal medicine man told him of the time he and several Indians were guiding a white prospector into the mountains.

They were sitting around the campfire one night when the ghost of old Slumach appeared, to warn the natives not to take the white man another step. "We left the prospector alone and returned," the old man recalled. "White man went no further. So he lived."

Something for interested treasure hunters to think about!

5

THE LOST PLATINUM CACHE

Does a bucket of platinum, said to be worth $50,000,
still lie buried among the ruins of Granite City?
Rumour persists that a Scandinavian named
Johannson buried such a hoard.

PLACER gold was known to exist in the Tulameen-Similkameen country since 1853, but, as a result of the fantastic yields of the Cariboo goldfields, its significance had gone relatively unnoticed. For a quarter of a century the rich gold-bearing creeks were only lightly worked by a mere handful of prospectors.

In July of 1885, however, all that changed. That was the month destiny chose to send a loafer named John Chance to the little flat opposite the, as yet unnamed, Granite Creek. Too lazy to work, Chance had been made a cook by the miners. However, as the hot summer days drew on, even this menial task proved too exhaustive. So, while others toiled under the blistering July sun, Chance grabbed his rifle and set off to bag a few grouse.

Saddling up, he plodded quietly along the banks of the Tulameen River. By noon the sun was shining fiercely, and when Chance stumbled across a cool mountain stream, he felt a rest was in order. Dismounting, he stretched out on the bank, dangled his feet in the cool water, and soon dozed off. When he awoke he noticed a yellow glint in the cool water. Reaching down, he extracted a solid gold nugget! Looking again, he found another and another, and soon his small buckskin pouch was bulging. When he returned to camp with the news, he suddenly became a hero and the "founder" of the boomtown of Granite City.

Within weeks a hodge-podge of tents dotted the little flat as hundreds of prospectors swarmed to the new diggings. The gold was shallow, plentiful and coarse, and nuggets were not uncommon. It was not long before the tents gave way to log buildings as the town of Granite City quickly began to take form. The next year, reported the Victoria *Colonist,* Granite City boasted

". . .9 general stores, 14 hotels and restaurants, 2 jewellers, 3 bakers, 3 blacksmiths, 2 livery stables, a shoemaker, butcher, chemist, doctor and 8 pack trains owned in the city." The main streets, Government and Granite were said to contain 200 buildings, although this is considered to be inaccurate. The population soon soared to 2,000 men and women as Granite City surpassed all British Columbia cities in size except Victoria and New Westminster.

Alas, Granite City's growth and prosperity were short-lived; when the gold began to peter out, so did the population. By 1896 most of the prospectors had drifted away, and many of the storekeepers had left. Buildings that had cost from $500 to $1,500 in labour and materials, were sold for $15 and used for fire-wood.

On April 4, 1907, fire broke out in the F.P. Cook store and quickly razed the town. Some buildings, including the Cook's store, were reconstructed, but it was too late — Granite City was doomed.

Today several buildings remain on the old townsite. One, the remains of the F.P. Cook store, stands near the cairn erected in memory of Johnny Chance's discovery. It, like the remaining buildings and townsite itself, has been scarred by the childish antics of vandals.

ORIGINAL LEGEND

When word of a new gold strike got out, prospectors swarmed to the area like flies around a molasses barrel. Prospectors and cowboys, reinforced by men from the Canadian Pacific Railway, soon had staked out nearly every foot of Granite Creek. Chinese and Whites toiled side by side at the new diggings, which at first seemed plentiful for all. The total recorded during the first year exceeded $100,000, with that amount more than doubled the following year.

However gold was not the only metal recovered from Granite Creek. A hard, silver-white, lustrous metal, comparable to gold in weight, also turned up in sluice boxes and gold pans. Separating gold from black sand was difficult enough, but separating gold from the equally heavy white metal proved to be a perplexing problem. The miners soon dubbed this nuisance metal "white gold," which at the time was considered worthless. Thus, at the close of each work day, many ounces of platinum were discarded like so much black sand.

Among the prospectors who staked a claim on Granite Creek, was a Scandinavian named Johansson, who arrived there around 1892-93. Unlike most, who considered "white gold" worthless, Johansson was fascinated by the strange metal. So, while others discarded it, Johansson collected and stored his in a baking powder tin. When word of his peculiar habit circulated through Granite City, the other miners, possibly as a joke, willingly offered Johansson their share of platinum. For two years Johansson

(Above) One of the few remaining buildings in Granite City in 1954.
(Below) A placer operation on the Tulameen River. More than a century after gold was discovered in the rivers of the Similkameen, miners continue to pursue the elusive deposits of gold, silver and platinum.

accumulated the platinum until at length, his small tin could hold no more. At this point, so the story goes, Johansson transferred his platinum to an old wooden water bucket which was said to have a 20-pound capacity.

By 1895, Granite Creek had been washed to the point where the gold was diminishing rapidly, and Johansson, like many others, decided to try his luck elsewhere. However when it came time to leave, Johansson realized he had accumulated a large quantity of "white gold." Considered worthless at the time, and very heavy, he decided to bury the platinum.

According to reports, the treasure site was purported to be within view of, and to the south of, his cabin door.

Contented that his platinum was safely hidden, Johansson departed Granite City, supposedly for the Kootenays, and never returned. Whatever became of him is not known, but Johansson was in his seventies, and it is believed he simply died of old age.

In any event, Johansson never returned for his platinum, and in a short while, everyone in Granite City forgot about the old water bucket and its silvery treasure. Then, several years later, when the price of platinum began to soar, memories were suddenly revived. In the intervening years, however, a fire had swept the town, and Johansson's log cabin, the only clue to the treasure, had been one of the first to burn. That did not deter the energies of the local residents, however, for they knew that somewhere beneath the scorched earth and ashes lay a fortune in platinum. Eagerly they searched for the old water bucket, but their efforts, like the efforts of many others down through the years, were not to be rewarded. So Granite City, now a shell of a town with only four broken log buildings, still guards the secret of Johansson's lost bucket of platinum.

SUMMARY AND CONCLUSION

There are only two known areas in the world where placer gold and platinum have been recovered side by side. One location is the Amur River in Russia, the other is the Tulameen-Similkameen River of British Columbia. Thus platinum was indeed known to exist in Granite Creek, and, by all indications, it existed in abundance. According to *Notes on Placer Mining, Bulletin #21*, platinum was "recovered with the placer gold from the Tulameen River and its producing tributaries, Granite, Cedar, Slate and Lawless (Bear) Creeks. In some places there is more platinum than gold. The platinum found is in nuggets up to half an ounce in weight. It is estimated that from 10,000 to 20,000 ounces of placer platinum has been recovered since 1885." Even as late as 1934, the *Minister of Mines* stated that 40 ounces of platinum were obtained by local merchants that year, and added: "Undoubtedly much more was sold elsewhere."

So the existence of placer platinum in and around the Granite

Creek area is undisputed. And Johansson, it would appear, was not the only one interested in the "white gold." The Chinese were also intrigued by it, and many were reported to have collected it. A letter received from a *Canadian Frontier* reader, Mr. M. McLeod, then 86, confirms these activities. Mr. McLeod had lived in Granite City and the surrounding district in the early 1900s. His letter, in part reads:

"The Chinese worked the Tulameen district many years ago. They found a lot of platinum with the gold, but at the time the price of platinum was so low (25¢ to 50¢ an ounce) that it was not worth carrying to New Westminster over the pony trail. The Chinese stored the platinum in baking powder cans and buried them under rocks around their cabins. Eventually they returned to China with their gold.

"During the depression one man made good money washing gold??? in the Tulameen. Some observed that he worked places where there was a fallen down old shack. He was a wise one and was searching for the tins of platinum left behind by the Chinese, as the price of the metal was high then. The theory was that he located some of this, and these were the values he found and not the gold he washed.

"Some time later, some old Chinese returned to Granite City to look for their platinum. They were tight-lipped and never revealed whether their search had been successful, but they did tell other Chinese that after 50 years the country had changed so much that they could not locate their cabins, for by that time they had rotted, or had been obliterated by fire."

McLeod's story confirms numerous other references that seem to prove conclusively that: (1) platinum was abundant in the district and, (2) Chinese miners collected it as a rule, rather than the exception.

Whether or not a Scandinavian named Johansson also amassed a large quantity of platinum is somewhat more difficult to prove, although the possibility certainly does exist. One aspect of the story, however, casts doubts on its existence. Much of the original legend is based on the premise that platinum was considered worthless by miners, and was given freely to Johansson. On the other hand, if platinum was known to be valuable, it is unlikely it would have been discarded by anyone. Lets examine that possibility.

Johansson was reputed to have collected his platinum from 1892-95, so those are the years we must be concerned with. Was platinum considered valuable or worthless during that period? The 1886 *Minister of Mines* states: "Mixed with gold found in this district, and possessed of a greater specific gravity, is a whitish metal which, at first, was thrown away under the impression that it was worthless. For a considerable time no definite idea could be

(Above) Granite City as it appeared in the early 1900s.
(Below) A general view of the remains of Granite City in 1984. The road in the middle leads back to Coalmont.

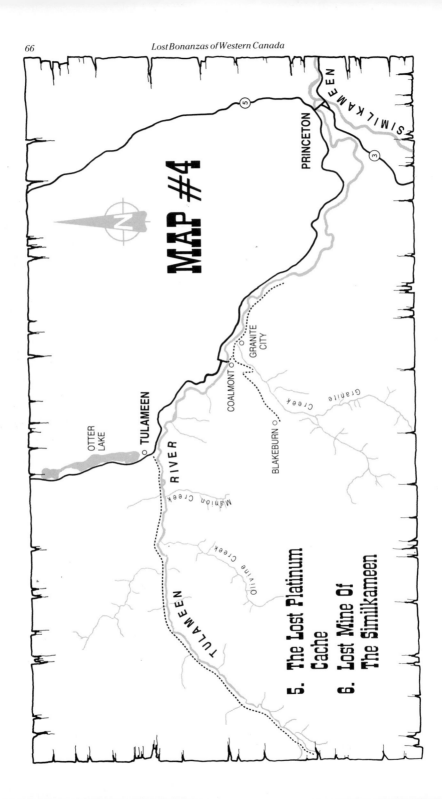

MAP #4

5. The Lost Platinum Cache
6. Lost Mine Of The Similkameen

Sootheran's Platinum Placers on the Tulameen River in 1926. Between May 17 and June 22, 35 ounces of platinum was taken out from short narrow drains and open-cuts over an area of about 200 feet. Since it came from old placer workings, it was assumed it had been ignored in earlier days.

procured as to its value. Mr. Jensen, of Granite City, who forwarded a sample to a cousin of his at Manchester, England, for analysis, has kindly supplied me with the desired information. The metal is principally platinum, containing small quantities of iridium, osmium, and palladium. Its value depends on the percentage of the platinum, which varies in quantity, and may be considered as worth about $2.50 per ounce. The selling price at Granite City was 50 cents per ounce; so the purchasers will reap a handsome return from this investment."

In 1888, the *Minister of Mines* recorded that 1,500 ounces of platinum had been recovered, and stated that its value had climbed to $3.50 per ounce.

In F.W. Howay's *British Columbia Historical,* published in 1914, the renown historian writes: "With the gold there was found a very hard, heavy, whitish metal, which was thought to be either platinum or iridium. Further examination proved it to be the former, and for years the Tulameen produced this rare metal in considerable quantities — in 1891, $10,000; in 1892, $3,500; in 1898, $1,500."

These references indicate that only during 1885 and part of 1886 was platinum considered worthless. Thenceforth, it was known to be valuable, and, in fact, steadily increased in value. It is highly unlikely, therefore, that the metal would have been given to Johannson or anyone else for free. In fact, the *Minister of Mines* for 1886 gives the impression that it was being purchased in Granite City for 50¢ an ounce and resold at $2.50.

However, another theory must also be considered: Perhaps the lost platinum cache, now said to be worth $50,000, blossomed around one of the baking powder tins said to be hidden in Granite City by the Chinese. Years of exaggerations by local residents could have magnified the treasure a hundredfold. In any event, provided they were not all recovered during the depression, there is a strong possibility that one or more of the baking powder tins might still be cached in Granite City. The hundreds of potholes discovered there during my visit in 1971, would indicate that there have been numerous searchers in the area. However most of these scars, I am sure, are merely the result of coin and relic hunters.

Hundreds of tourists visit Granite City each summer: some come simply to enjoy the scenery; others search for relics and bottles. Perhaps one day someone will stumble across a decaying old water bucket and discover a cache of platinum that has eluded treasure hunters for nearly 100 years. That same platinum that was once considered worthless, is now valued at over $500 an ounce!

The grave of F.P. Cook in the Granite City cemetery. Cook operated a general store in Granite City, the ruins of which still stand today.

6

LOST MINE
OF THE SIMILKAMEEN

On striking a match, they found bones scattered all over the tunnel. Were they the remains of the missing prospectors? If they were, this was where they made their last stand against an unknown enemy.

GEORGE B. McClellan first discovered gold in the Similkameen River in 1853. Unfortunately, it was only in small amounts, and it was not until 1860 that regular placer-mining was carried on along the bars of the Similkameen. In the fall of that year, on a flat bordering the river about seven miles south of Princeton, at least 100 American and Chinese miners established a small community called Blackfoot.

In 1861, however, Williams and Lightning, the two most celebrated creeks in the annals of B.C. placer mining, were discovered in the Cariboo. These newest goldfields quickly depopulated the Similkameen district of its white miners, and there is no further mention of mining activity in the region until 1885. For the 25 years in between only a few Chinese remained along the Similkameen. But they contented themselves with known producing areas, not bothering to prospect untried creeks. Thus, to their dismay, the golden riches of Granite Creek, Tulameen River and its tributaries lay hidden and undisturbed until discovered by John Chance in 1885.

Over the Hope Mountains, with toboggans and snowshoes, men crowded into the new goldfields. By the end of October, 1885, the first five miles of Granite Creek was staked and 62 companies were at work. The Point Company obtained $750 as the results of eight men's work for 30 hours; another — Briggs & Bromley — $400 in one afternoon. Before the year was out new discoveries were made on Britton (Eagle) Creek, Collins Gulch, Lawless (Bear) Creek, Lockie (Boulder) Creek and others, and the prospects for a massive goldfield looked bright. Unfortunately, the peak years lasted only a decade, from 1885-1895, after which production steadily decreased.

ORIGINAL LEGEND

In the summer of 1856, a party of American prospectors made their way into the mountains at the head of the Similkameen River, where they remained all summer. When they returned that fall, they showed very rich gold specimens to a man named Walker, who, at that time, was the only white settler on the Similkameen River. They told him that they had found a very rich gold quartz vein, but would not provide further information.

In 1857, a much larger party of prospectors, with a large pack train, returned. Once more they headed north, only this time they did not return, and it would be many years before the "supposed" location of their mine would be found. In fact, had it not been for an Indian woman, it might never have been found at all.

This Indian woman was the wife of remittance man Horace Parker Manley, more popularly referred to as "Parkey." Parkey enjoyed his Hudson's Bay Rum, and it seemed to take all the funds sent to him by friends at home to keep his throat quenched. Parkey was a bit of an outcast, and whenever his entourage entered the mining camp the miners, for the most part, ignored them. But Parkey did have one friend in camp, an Irishman named Mike Widrow. Unlike Parkey, Widrow was not of noble extraction, but he was a good worker, a hard fighter and a good drinking man. Perhaps the fact that Widrow, like Parkey, had an Indian wife accounted for their friendship. In any event, the friends would celebrate freely whenever Parkey's remittance arrived or Widrow made a strike.

But there were also many days of drought, and it was during one such lean period that Parkey's wife remembered the legend of the lost mine. Her grandfather, now very old, used to boast that he knew where the lost mine was located. Furthermore, he hinted vaguely that he knew what had happened to the white men who discovered it.

Legends of lost mines did nothing for the aristocratic mind of Parkey, but it fired the mining instincts of Widrow, who used to say: "if it panned out all right we could buy enough rum to float a ship." So they decided to seek out the source of information — the grandfather.

Indians are usually adverse to giving whites information that will lead to their finding mines. However this time the old man agreed to direct the group to the lost mine. Feeble and old, he had to be carried by younger Indians.

Leading them to a small creek, evidently an affluent of the Tulameen River, the old Indian declared the area infested with evil spirits, and he refused to go further. But he did give directions. The white men were to follow the creek up until they came to a place where the water raised "hiyu." By climbing to the top they would find a small bench covered with white rocks where a cabin had once stood. Although the cabin had been burned to the ground a long time ago, a careful search would reveal where it had stood. Then, by looking directly across the creek, they would see a hole in the mountain — that was the place.

Bidding farewell to the old man and the other Indians, Parkey and Widrow started out on their trek. They had no difficulty locating the site described by the old Indian. Although the mouth of the adit had caved in, and debris from the mountain had covered up the old workings, there was still a small passage by which they could get into the tunnel. Investigating around the entrance, they discovered the remains of an old forge and piles of rusted iron that must have been tools. The mine itself looked old and decayed, and its ghostly appearance caused an uneasiness among the two men. Perhaps it was this uneasiness that prevented them from rushing immediately into the mine. In any event, if they needed encouragement, it came suddenly when Widrow picked up a piece of rock, which, to his joy and surprise, was laced with free gold.

Both men now rushed for the adit, scrambling over the fallen debris to get into the tunnel. Here, an even greater surprise awaited them. On striking a light and looking around, they found human bones scattered all over the tunnel. They were able to count seven skulls, which indicated at least seven individuals had perished here. Were these the remains of the lost prospectors? If so, then this was where they had made their last stand against an enemy.

Eventually overcoming their nervousness, the two men continued to the head of the tunnel where they found a well-defined ledge some four feet in width. Nine or 10 inches of this width contained quartz that literally sparkled with free gold. Breaking off a few rich samples, the two men returned to daylight.

As night was fast approaching, they made camp and cooked supper, after which they excitedly examined the specimens and speculated on the richness of their discovery. It was so rich, they expected to recover a small fortune with a hand dolly before selling the mine for millions. With his share, Parkey would return to England, buy himself an estate and perhaps work himself into a peerage. Widrow was not quite as ambitious. He would content himself with owning a sporting house in San Francisco, where he would keep fighting dogs and game chickens. Finally, exhausted by the days events, the two settled into a sound, restful sleep.

Sometime during the night they were startled by a yell so loud that it brought them to their feet in an instant. Before they were able to determine where the yell came from, it was repeated, followed by Indian war whoops, while the ground seemed to tremble beneath the rush of many feet. Then the sharp report of firearms seemed to come from where the old cabin had stood. The air was filled with groans and yells; they were in the midst of a battle — a battle fought by ghostly combatants. Flesh and blood could not stand this, so they made a head-long dash down the

canyon, stumbling and falling over rocks.

About 10 days later a little procession entered the town of Granite City. It consisted of two squaws, two papooses, an old Indian and two nondescripts, clothed in squaw blankets. While the squaws and their papooses sunned themselves, the men entered the Miner's Rest Saloon in search of spirituous comfort. At first the barkeeper refused to serve these "Indians." It was only after Widrow threw off his blanket, exposing his nearly nude body, and threatening to fight, that his right to the poison was established.

Smacking his lips with evident relish, Widrow turned and faced the people in the small saloon. "Boys, I lost my clothes and came near losing my life, but I saved the pocket of my jumper, and that holds quartz specimens that will make your eyes bulge when you see them."

When he dumped the rich specimens on the counter, every man who saw them felt envious of the unfortunates who found them. Widrow then described how they had found the mine but were driven away by ghosts. But, ghost or no ghost, the specimens were real enough, solid evidence that they had found a mine.

A party of miners was soon made up to go out and reclaim it. This party was to be guided by Parkey and Widrow, who were to retain half interest in the mine, and to share evenly with the other miners in any other claims that might be discovered. In consideration of this agreement, the miners were to furnish tools, provisions and liquids.

While these preparations were underway, an addition was made to the party. This "very necessary" addition was none other that Father John. Father John was quite a character. He had founded a mission on the Prairies on a grant of land obtained from the Canadian government. Through the assistance of Indian labour, Father John greatly increased the value of this land. Everything went fine until the church asked Father John to turn over the property. Father John refused, stating that the original grant had been in his brother's name and that his brother had conveyed it to him. Accused of robbing the church, Father John was never again trusted with any other mission or church business. So, with the proceeds from the sale of the mission property, Father John drifted west to the gold mines.

When he learned of the enterprise, Father John said: "Boys, you are embarking on a very dangerous expedition. You are about to invade a piece of territory that the good Lord has seen fit to hand over to the forces of darkness. That these forces will resent your intrusion is evident from the manner in which they received the visit of Mike and Parkey. Ordinary miners and ordinary weapons

The Similkameen Valley. Somewhere in the distant mountains, according to legend, a lost gold mine awaits rediscovery.

are useless in fighting such an enemy. Now what you want is a man clothed in the strong armor of the church. I am that man and I am here to serve you, and all I ask is an even share in the enterprise with the rest of you."

"What a nose you have for scenting out a good thing," said Ned Barrow.

"Oh! he's not here for his health," said old Pat Synon.

Father John's lips curled, and he was about to rebuke the old man, when he was interrupted by Lawrence Hays, who was the secretary of the company. "Father John, you are always receiving money and you never spend any, you must have a tidy wad stowed away. So, if you want an interest in our company you can pay for it."

Father John made another appeal, however, telling them that although he had neither goods nor gold to enrich the company with, he had something of far more value, to-wit; a bottle of Ghost Medicine. After some more spiritual consultation, he was finally received into the company as ghost-killer and next morning a start was made for the new El Dorado.

The party made such good progress that before nightfall camp had been made on "Turn Back Bobby" Creek, some 30 miles from Granite City. After supper, pipes were lit, followed by the appearance of a demijohn full of McCarthy's best, and the evening was enlivened by songs and tales of deeds of daring.

One by one the singers and story tellers fell back on the grass and went to sleep. Murphy, who had imbibed more than a fair share of the bug juice, woke up during the night. Consumed with a burning thirst, he found two bottles under a tree. They contained water, or a fluid that tasted like water. Shortly after he finished the second bottle, however, he became sick and began retching. After a great deal of vomiting, he felt better and went back to sleep.

When he awoke at daybreak the camp was in an anxious state. Father John was rampaging around like a mad bull while the rest of the men looked very despondent. As Murphy arose to his feet, Father John approached him and asked: "Murphy, do you know what became of the ghost medicine that was under the tree?"

"Ghost medicine," exclaimed Murphy, "well that accounts for it."

"Accounts for what?" rejoined Father John in a stern voice.

"Why," said Murphy, "I drank it, and it came near killing me, but I thought it was water."

The only thing to do was to turn back and wait until Father John could get a fresh supply of medicine. But while waiting, Mike and Parkey would have to be looked after so that they would not be tempted to reveal the secret to anybody else. To this end they were furnished with a liberal supply of grub and tobacco, to which was added a keg of HBC rum.

Two nights after the keg had been landed at Squaw Flats, Parkey's wife rushed into the Miner's Rest saloon, crying aloud in her distress that "Mike heap mamaloosed Parkey." At first those in the saloon thought she meant simply that Mike and Parkey had settled a difference of opinion through fisticuffs. But after she calmed down, she explained that Mike had attacked Parkey with an axe, and that Parkey was dead. This sent a cold chill through those present, but their action was prompt and to the point.

Const. "Stumpy McGinnis" was called from the back room where he was engaged in a poker game. A posse was hastily gathered and the men headed for the scene of the tragedy. On their arrival, they found Parkey dead but Mike was nowhere to be found.

A search of the premises showed that the keg or rum was missing, indicating that Mike had taken it with him. This was verified, for when a helpless Mike was overtaken at Four Mile Creek, the keg was at his side.

Mike was taken to the county seat to be tried before Judge Baccus, better known as "Old Hang 'em," and six weeks later he was hanged.

Father John stayed with Mike until the last. Many felt that he did this only in the hopes of obtaining some clue as to the location of the mine. Father John did make excursions into the mountains every year, but each time he returned empty-handed. Thus it would appear that he was merely trying to re-discover the mine based on the sketchy information that was available. He never succeeded and, neither apparently, did anyone else.

SUMMARY & CONCLUSION

Of all the treasure stories in this book, this is truly the will-o-the-wisp. Almost nothing can be substantiated as factual. Of all the individuals named — Walker, Horace Parker Manley, Mike Widrow, Father John, Ned Barrow, Pat Synon, Lawrence Hays, Murphy, Const. "Stumpy McGinnis" and Judge Baccus — not one can be positively identified. The first person to write about this lost mine was "Judge" Thomas C. Murphy. He was a longtime Granite Creek resident whose quarters, along with the celebrated Cariboo House, were the only buildings in town to survive the 1907 fire. Is he also the Murphy in the story?

Judge Baccus should be easy to verify. Unfortunately, there is no mention of a Judge Baccus in B.C. history. The reference to him as "Old Hang 'em" deepens the mystery. The celebrated Judge Begbie was known as the "Hanging Judge." Is Judge Baccus suppose to be Judge Begbie? If so, why the change in name?

The story dangles some tantalizing clues to the mine's location: Turn Back Bobby Creek; 30 miles from Granite City; and a branch of the Tulameen River. Unfortunately, I have not been able to locate a creek called "Turn Back Bobby." It not only does not exist in the Tulameen area, there is no reference to it in any of the *Minister of Mines Reports.*

The original legend states that samples of the rich ore were first

Both the Tulameen General Store and Dominion Hotel, shown here in the early 1970s, have disappeared. Each stood in Tulameen City on the shore of Otter Lake.

(Above) An early view of Granite City with "Frenchys" cabin in foreground.
(Below) This shallow mine at Granite City is of more recent vintage.

shown "to a man named Walker, who, at that time, was the only white settler on the Similkameen River." In actual fact, John Fall Allison was the first permanent settler in the Similkameen Valley. He had a ranch near Princeton, which, incidentally, was first named Allison, in his honour. It was later named Vermillion Forks, then, finally, Princeton. Allison's ranch became a place of call to everyone travelling through the region. In later years Allison became Assistant Gold Commissioner for the Similkameen district.

We know that Granite City existed, and that, since its peak years were 1885-95, this story, if true, would probably have taken place during that period. The reference to Squaw Flats is unquestionably Otter Flats. Otter Lake had long been the home of the Tulameen Indians, whose village became known as *Campement des Femmes* (Camp of Women). Otter Flats became a regular campsite for the HBC brigades between 1849 and 1860. Today the site is the town of Tulameen.

And then we have the ghosts. While Indians were often superstitious of spirits, I find it impossible to believe that a party of white miners would be frightened by the "possibility" of encountering ghosts, and giving up on the prospects of such a valuable mine. Similarly, it is very convenient for the only two people who know the mine's location to be eliminated.

In the extremely remote possibility that this lost mine exists, it would be probably be located in the headwaters of the Tulameen River. Two clues lead to that assumption. First, the original prospectors went north into the headwaters of the Similkameen, and second, Parkey and Widrow made their discovery on a branch of the Tulameen. A glance at a map of the area quickly reveals that the headwaters of the Similkameen and Tulameen rivers rise in the same mountainous region only a few miles apart. If, through extensive research, someone could identify a small creek as "Turn Back Bobby," this story might then have some merit.

In the absence of such a discovery, however, and with so little supportive evidence to go on, this lost mine must be, for the moment at least, considered pure bunkum. There are much more promising treasures, to be sure.

7

THE LOST GOLD BARS OF CAMP McKINNEY

In August, 1896, three gold bricks en route to Midway were stolen by a lone bandit. Although the suspected robber was later killed, the gold, now worth about $275,000, was never recovered.

GOLD was first discovered on Rock Creek in 1858. The honour fell to a Canadian by the name of Adam Beam, although there are many who insist that gold was discovered there a year earlier, in 1857, by two American soldiers. In any event, the area was soon swarming with prospectors and a minor gold rush was on. As the gold began to play out, however, many of the original prospectors began drifting from the area. Those who remained began panning nearby creeks and streams in the hopes of making new discoveries.

The history of Camp McKinney began in 1884 when two placer miners named Goericke and Runnels discovered the Victoria vein on Rock Creek a short distance above the placer diggings of earlier days. But it was not until 1887, when Al McKinney and Fred Rice located the Cariboo vein at the 4,600-foot-level of the southeast slope of Bald Mountain that Camp McKinney, British Columbia's first lode camp, began to take shape around the Cariboo-Amelia mine. Soon shacks and log cabins sprang up along its dusty single street, and Hugh Cameron's Saloon and Hotel graced the scene.

Later, James Monahan and George McAuley of Spokane purchased the mine from McKinney and Rice, and made Joseph P. Keane their superintendent. In 1894 Monahan imported a 10-stamp mill from Washington, and before long the mine was prospering.

Camp McKinney was isolated and could only be reached by two roads; one from Anarchist Mountain, known as Sidley Road, the other, from the Okanagan, known as the Fairview Road. These roads converged about two miles from town. The only connection between Camp McKinney and the outside world was Snodgrass' six-horse stage, which ran through the camp on its way from Penticton to Marcus, Washington, two or three times a week.

This painting by the author depicts Camp McKinney's main street in the late 1890s.

(Above) According to legend, the buckboard carrying the gold shipment was always accompanied by guards. In actual fact, the shipment was carried out as if it was "so much yellow bacon."

(Left) Chief Const. William McMynn. After examining the evidence, he was convinced Keane had murdered Roderick, and sent a letter outlining those suspicions to Dep. Aty.-Gen. Arthur Smith.

(Below) These miners passed the hat to help pay the ailing Roderick's passage back to Seattle. When the gold shipment was robbed, they joined the posse searching for their larcenous coworker. The log cabin was the Cariboo mine's bunk and boarding house.

Once every month or two, the gold that had accumulated at the mine was melted into bars and taken by wagon to Midway. From there it was transshipped to the San Francisco mint. Out story of stolen bullion revolves around one of these shipments.

ORIGINAL LEGEND

It was on the bright morning of August 18, 1896, that George McAuley climbed into the buckboard at Camp McKinney. Visiting for a few days from Spokane, McAuley had opted to replace Keane, who usually made the trip to Midway. Ignoring the usual precaution of an armed guard, he headed out of town. On the floorboards behind him, concealed in saddlebags, were three gold bars with a combined weight of 656½ ounces. At the going price of $20 an ounce paid in those days, the shipment was valued at just over $13,000.

As the sun rose over the mountains, McAuley found himself moving leisurely among the Jack pines that flanked the narrow mountain road. The sky was clear and the wind light. In a few hours the heat of midday would drench him in sweat, so McAuley was making the most of the fresh morning air.

Two or three miles from Camp McKinney, as he rounded a sharp turn near McMynn's Meadows, a masked man suddenly stepped out of the bushes. Brandishing a Winchester, the highwayman ordered McAuley to stop and throw down the saddlebags. McAuley may have been foolish for leaving town without an armed escort, but he was not completely stupid. He could see the obvious disadvantage of arguing with a loaded rifle, and promptly handed over the bullion.

"Now drive on and don't turn back," warned the robber.

Whipping the team to a gallop, McAuley proceeded down the trail for about a mile. When he found a spot wide enough to turn the buckboard, he hastened back to town to spread the alarm.

When Monahan was notified of the robbery, his first act was to check on all mining personnel. Everyone was present and accounted for. Monahan then sent McAuley for the Provincial Police stationed at Midway, while he quickly organized a posse. However, although Monahan's group searched the robbery scene and nearby woods, they were unsuccessful in unearthing any leads.

Later that afternoon, constables William G. McMynn and Isaac Dinsmore arrived at Camp McKinney. After asking some routine questions they proceeded to the scene of the robbery. It was Dinsmore who apparently discovered the empty saddle bags and whiskey bottles that had been overlooked by the Monahan search party earlier. These articles shed no new light on the mystery, however.

There was nothing substantial to go on, and for some time no new leads were uncovered. Although it was considered impossible for a robber to flee the area undetected, many felt that he had somehow made a clean getaway. To apprehend the culprit, rewards totalling $3,500 were posted by the mining company — $2,000 for the arrest and conviction of the guilty party, and $1,500 for the recovery of the stolen bullion.

It was not long before the enticement of reward money provided the Company with their first big break. It came in the form of a letter addressed to Monahan. Later published in the November 14, 1896 issue of the Grand Forks *Miner,* it was written by a man named Shuttleworth.

"I met a man in a saloon in Oroville at about the end of May. We fell to drinking together and he told me that his name was Mathew Roderick, from Spokane, that he was very hard up and on his way to get the bullion from Camp McKinney — an easy job he said.

"He had a gun, a Winchester I think, and was going to stage a holdup. He liked the way I held my liquor — said I'd be one with a cool head and wanted me to come in with him on the job. I didn't want to. Roderick said he was a dead shot and he wouldn't hesitate to kill me if I revealed what passed between us that night.

"We went to Camp McKinney where we both got work. After we had been working three months, and nothing happened, I left for Trail Creek late in August. After I'd been there three days I read an account of the robbery of the Camp McKinney bullion in the 'Spokesman Review,' so I thought I'd better let you know about Roderick."

Monahan did some quick checking and soon confirmed that a man name Roderick had indeed been employed at the mine during the time of the robbery. His investigation revealed that Roderick had not been a model worker; that each week after he collected his pay he would indulge in one of the continuous poker games held at Hugh Cameron's Saloon. Since Roderick never left the game until he was broke, he often ignored his shift for two or three days at a time.

Roderick had lived in a small cabin on the outskirts of town. On the day of the robbery, and for a few days previous, he had been absent from work due to a bad back, and had been observed hobbling around the camp with the aid of a home-made crutch. Sympathetic miners had occasionally brought him whiskey, fruit and eggs. A few days after the robbery, Roderick decided to return to his Seattle home to recuperate. The miners, feeling sorry for him, had passed a hat and collected $84 to pay for his passage home. Those who remembered seeing him leave were certain he had taken only his blanket with him. (In those days it was recognized as a sign of respectability for a man to travel with his own blankets.)

The Cariboo Mining Company promptly enlisted the services of a Pinkerton Detective Agency in Washington to place Roderick

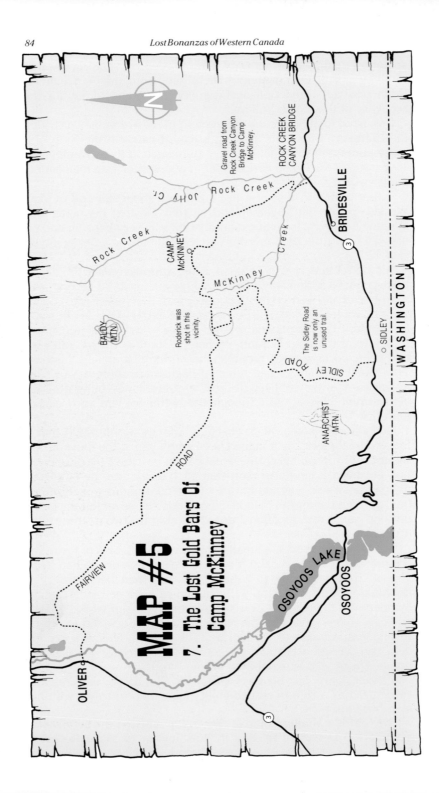

MAP #5
7. The Lost Gold Bars Of Camp McKinney

Gravel road from Rock Creek Canyon Bridge to Camp McKinney.

ROCK CREEK CANYON BRIDGE

BRIDESVILLE

Rock Creek

Roderick was shot in this vicinity.

CAMP McKINNEY

McKinney Creek

BALDY MTN.

The Sidley Road is now only an unused trail.

SIDLEY ROAD

SIDLEY

WASHINGTON

ANARCHIST MTN.

FAIRVIEW ROAD

OSOYOOS LAKE

OSOYOOS

OLIVER

Abandoned mine workings at Camp McKinney in 1984. (Inset) The mineshaft of the Cariboo-Amelia mine.

under surveillance. They had no difficulty locating him at 329 Taylor St. in Seattle, as he was listed in the directory as a civil engineer. Investigations soon revealed that, since returning home from British Columbia, Roderick had paid up his back taxes and had taken out a $3,000 insurance policy — a neat trick for a man who had supposedly left Camp McKinney broke!

All the evidence seemed to indicate that Roderick was their man, but the mining company was primarily interested in recovering the bullion, so they decided to adopt a wait and see attitude. They felt certain Roderick had managed to smuggle out the smaller bar valued at $1,600, in the bedroll; but they were equally convinced that he had hidden the two larger bars in the general vicinity of Camp McKinney.

As part of their investigations, the Pinkertons had a woman detective move in next door to the Rodericks. As neighbours will, she soon struck up a friendly acquaintance with Mrs. Roderick, who, the detective reported, apparently knew nothing about her husband's illegal enterprise. She believed her husband had made a rich strike in the British Columbia goldfields. Then one day the unsuspecting Mrs. Roderick advised the detective that her husband was preparing to leave on a business trip — "one that will make us rich," she said.

Unaware that he was being followed, Roderick travelled by train to Loomis, Washington, where he purchased a grey saddle-horse and rode north for the B.C. boundary.

Camp McKinney, meanwhile, feverishly prepared for his arrival. Armed men were positioned at strategic vantage points around Bald Mountain, guarding every approach. Tom Graham, and an Indian called Alexine (or Long Alex), were hidden at the forks of the Sidley and Fairview roads. From their vantage point they commanded an excellent view of the surrounding countryside.

On the evening of October 26, 1896, the suspect was observed by Graham making his way up the mountain road toward them. Alexine was immediately dispatched to Camp McKinney to give the alarm. Two provincial constables, Louis Cuppage and R.W. Dean, were in Hugh Cameron's Saloon with Superintendent Keane when the Indian burst in with the news. Arming themselves, Dean and Keane set off down the trail. It was then about 10 p.m. Outside thick clouds obscured the moon in what was later reported as "one of the blackest nights of the year."

The small party had been walking about a mile when they noticed some object on the road; however, the pitch darkness made identification impossible. After walking a bit farther, they realized that is was a horse.

The men stopped and waited, and in the silence that followed, Keane was heard to ask, "Is that you, Matt?"

There was no further sound for perhaps half a minute, then the silence was shattered by a shot. Dean, fearing Roderick had felled Keane, fired his rifle at the figure of a man he had glimpsed in the flash of the initial shot. His shot was expended for nothing, however, for it had been Keane's weapon that had spoken previously. His bullet had entered Roderick just below the left chest, penetrated the heart, and lodged in the back muscles. Dean's shot had been fired at the already dead, falling body of Roderick.

Roderick's rifle, which Keane later testified had been aimed at him, was found to contain a rag stuffed in the muzzle. Both it, and the pistol recovered from the body, were coated with rust. A small amount of money was also found on the body. Under Roderick's coat was discovered a special vest with two pockets, one under each armpit, large enough to accommodate the two large gold bars. There was no sign of the bullion, however, and it was believed that Roderick was returning to his secret cache when he was killed.

A coroner's inquest into Roderick's death was held at Camp McKinney on October 28, 1896, by Dr. Jakes of Greenwood. The jury, composed of H. Nicolson, foreman; J. Attwood, W.H. Blick, George Bennet, A. Cosens and V.R. Swanson, decided it was a case of "justifiable homicide," and absolved Keane of all blame.

SUMMARY AND CONCLUSION

Despite reports and claims by various writers that the McKinney bullion shipments were "shrouded in secrecy" and "escorted under armed guards," this was not the case at all. For proof of this we refer to two newspapers of that period.

Grand Forks *Miner,* August 22, 1896. "These shipments have been made regularly for months past, and the public always knew within a day or two of the exact time at which they would pass through, so that the only surprise created by the holdup is that it had not happened before."

The *Province,* September 5, 1896. "The robbers' success is not in any way a cause for surprise. What is astonishing is that ere this some enterprising scoundrel had not had a try at 'raising the wind' at the expense of so small an amount of labour or difficulty. Ever since gold was first produced from the Cariboo Mine, bullion had been carried out as if it were of no more value than so much yellow bacon, without the slightest care or precaution being taken to guard for its arrival at its destination."

So much for the reported secrecy and security. Another point which many writers seem to disagree on, is who actually drove the buckboard that fateful morning 92 years ago, McAuley or Keane. For the record, it was McAuley; a fact once again verified by the same issue of the *Province* newspaper mentioned above: "Mr. G.B. McAuley, of Spokane, secretary of the Cariboo Mining Company, was 'held up' by a masked robber on his return from the mine in charge of three gold bricks. . . ."

Researchers are also in disagreement on precisely what actions

McAuley followed immediately after the robbery. Some writers claim he drove the buckboard to C.W. Hozier's farm and sent Mr. Hozier's son back to Camp McKinney to give the alarm. Another account states that he proceeded to H. Pittendrich's Hotel at Rock Creek, while still another is convinced he raced directly to Midway to notify the Provincial Police. A fourth version, and one that appears more likely, is the one used in this story. However, it is impossible to determine at this late date which course of action he actually did take, and since the matter is of little consequence to the eventual outcome of the story, the reader may choose his own version.

Some writers claim that candles, matches and goggles were taken from Roderick's body shortly after his death. Accordingly, they suggest that he buried the stolen bullion in one of the old water-filled shafts. This could not be confirmed, however it appears highly unlikely that Roderick would go to such elaborate measures to hide the gold when he was pressed for time. It seems far more likely that he would have buried it in a convenient, safe spot that would be easily accessible to him; some place outside of town where his actions would not draw suspicion.

Of the numerous treasure stories I have read, researched or analysed, I have always believed that this one had an excellent chance of existing. It's a matter of record and undisputed fact that the robbery took place and the gold was never recovered, It has always been assumed that Roderick managed to smuggle out the smaller bar worth $1.600. If indeed he did, then the unrecovered bullion would have a value of just over $275,000 at present day prices. However, almost everyone assumes that Roderick was the robber, and that he was returning to recover his loot when shot and killed. But was he? Recently, I uncovered some documentation which deepens the mystery surrounding the Camp McKinney gold bars.

The first is a letter written by Chief Const. William McMynn to Dep. Att.-Gen. Arthur Smith on October 30, 1896, four days after Roderick was shot. In his letter, McMynn stated that Keane was arrested for shooting Roderick and appeared before a Coroner's Inquest on October 28. At the inquest, Keane was absolved of all blame, the verdict stating: "That the said Matt Roderick met his death at the hands of J.P. Keane by a .38 calibre pistol bullet on the night of the 26th day of October instant 1896 at Camp McKinney in the County aforesaid, and that the said J.P. Keane acted justifiably in self defence." McMynn accordingly released Keane, but asked Smith if he was ". . .required to take any further steps in this matter against Mr. Keane?"

Upon receiving McMynn's letter, Smith wrote to Supt. of Police F.S. Hussey on November 6. Although that letter has not survived, I do have a copy of Hussey's reply to Smith dated November 14.

Camp McKinney's Sailor Hotel.

In that letter Hussey explains that he has read the report of Coroner Jakes and McMynn, and after looking carefully into the matter, "...have ordered the arrest and prosecution of J.P. Keane for murder." This charge was eventually reduced to manslaughter, for which Keane went to trial in Vernon in June, 1897. Found guilty, the judge, Chief Justice McCall said: "You have been found guilty in a technical and legal sense," and sentenced him to one day in jail. Having already served this time, Keane was released and the matter closed.

But was this entire incident so cut and dried? Was Roderick the actual robber? Did he act alone if he was? Was he shot in self defence as Keane claims? Although these and many other questions remain unanswered, a letter written by Brady & Gay, the Seattle law firm representing Mrs. Roderick, if nothing else, muddies the water a bit. The letter gives us a new perspective into the entire incident. For example, we have been led to believe Roderick was a hard-drinking gambler who frequently missed work, whereas the letter describes him as a family man with children, "peaceable and law-abiding, sober and industrious." Likewise, the legend states Roderick, unaware he was being followed, was sneaking back to Camp McKinney to recover his stolen gold. If this letter can be believed, however, Roderick was not only aware he was a suspect, but knew he was being watched by detectives. Furthermore, rather than return to Camp McKinney in secrecy, Roderick had actually announced that he was going there on business.

The events surrounding Roderick's death are not what we have been led to believe either. According to the legend, Keane was supposed to have been accompanied by Dean on the fateful night of the shooting. However, the letter states it was Graham who accompanied Keane. If the letter is correct, and Graham did hide behind a stump, he was not in a position to know exactly what happened between Keane and Roderick, thereby leaving Keane's version of the encounter the only one available. Keane, of course, said he fired in self defence, however we know now that this was not true, at least according to the Court which convicted him of manslaughter. So we are left with some nagging doubts.

We know Roderick's weapons were unloaded so he would not have made any threatening motions towards Keane. But we do not know if Keane, in his own mine, felt threatened and obligated to fire? Did Keane believe Roderick to be a dangerous felon and simply shoot prematurely without malice? Was the killing of Roderick a tragic overreaction on the part of Keane, or were his motives more sinister? Remember, Constable McMynn, Coroner Jakes, Dep. Att.-Gen. Smith, Superintendent Hussey and the Seattle law firm of Brady & Gay all considered the shooting a murder, and that assumption was based on evidence available at the time.

Did Keane intentionally murder Roderick, and if so, why? One theory might be that Roderick, if he was the robber, was in partnership with Keane. If so, that partnership was terminated abruptly on the evening of October 26. Fascinating questions and theories all, but questions for which we will likely never learn the answers.

If Roderick was indeed the robber, and remember, it has never been proven that he was, he was probably returning for his stolen gold. Since he was killed before recovering it, where is its likely hiding place? The most likely area can be narrowed down to an area one-half mile on either side of the road between the townsite of Camp McKinney and the forks of the Sidley-Fairview roads, which converged about two miles from town. However, this is still a considerable area to search for a treasure that has been lost for 92 years.

Camp McKinney is deserted now; even its ghosts are gone. Only a few piles of decaying lumber, some abandoned shafts, and the occasional log cabin back in the forest mark its passing.

A dusty, but good, gravel road leads through the Camp McKinney site from the Rock Creek Canyon bridge. It passes through the scattered ruins, reminiscent of the days of old when miner's picks rang through the mountains and poker games lasted for days on end. Enjoy the quiet solitude, and wander among the Jack pines that hold the secret to the Lost Gold Bars of Camp McKinney.

8

JOLLY JACK'S
LOST PLACER

*Is the mysterious source of John "Jolly Jack" Thornton's
gold still waiting to be discovered, or has its location
finally been traced through the investigation
and research of historian N.L. Barlee?*

BOUNDARY Creek was found to be auriferous as early as 1862. Because of its spottiness, however, it was not until May, 1886, that the first claim was staked by W.T. Smith. By 1892, miners were active along the creek, which, south of the falls was exceptionally rich in places. The following year, however, with the exception of a single miner, Boundary Creek lay abandoned.

The one miner who persevered was John "Jolly Jack" Thornton, who "on July 27th applied for 300 inches of water at three cents for mining purposes." According to the *Minister of Mines* report, he was still there in 1894: "Boundary Creek seems, as far as placer mining is concerned, to be virtually abandoned. The last claim on the creek, the Louisa, held by Mr. John Thornton, lapsed on May last." Regardless of his claim having lapsed, Thornton had built a 500-foot wingdam and was still sluicing the ground.

Born at Stockton-on-Tees, County of Durham, England, on June 11, 1824, Thornton became a sailor at a very early age. In 1838 he left home to become an apprentice on a collier, and for the next six years he voyaged here, there and everywhere. After having "sailed the Spanish Main" Thornton landed in the United States, and thereafter sailed out of New York, Philadelphia, New Orleans and other Atlantic ports to the West Indies, Venezuela and Bermuda.

In 1844 Thornton joined the United States Navy (USN), serving aboard the steam frigate *Princeton,* the first vessel in the USN to have a propeller. After being discharged two years later, Thornton returned to the merchant service, and in 1846 was sailing on the *Commodore Shoebrink* out of Boston. From Boston Thornton went to California, for the Mexican War was in progress; but by the time

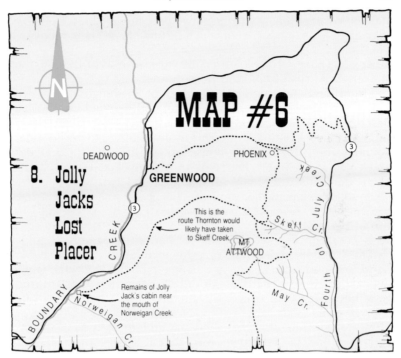

MAP #6

8. Jolly Jacks Lost Placer

DEADWOOD

PHOENIX

GREENWOOD

This is the route Thornton would likely have taken to Skeff Creek

MT. ATTWOOD

Remains of Jolly Jack's cabin near the mouth of Norweigan Creek.

Norweigan Cr.

CREEK

BOUNDARY

Skeff Cr.

July Creek

to Fourth

May Cr.

he reached San Francisco the Stars and Stripes had already been hoisted.

Thornton returned to New York around the Horn in the frigate *Savannah*. For the next four years he shipped on a number of merchant vessels and was again drafted in the USN, serving on the frigate *Rareton*. Discharged at New York, Thornton shipped on board the brig *Meteor* around the Horn to Valparaiso, Chili.

It was while in Valparaiso that word reached Thornton in 1848 about the new gold discoveries in California. Thornton immediately joined the Scotch brig *Annie Moore* and sailed for San Francisco. For nine years he tried his luck in the California goldfields. At one point, having been buried by a fall of earth, he was out of commission for nearly a year.

When gold was discovered on the Fraser River in 1858, Thornton joined the thousands of Californians into the area. When late arrivals were confronted with high water which prevented access to the gold, many declared the Fraser River a "humbug" and returned home. Thornton, however, headed into the Boundary Country, arriving in the Rock Creek area sometime in 1859. A wanderer, Thornton next moved on to the Columbia River below

Boundary Creek in 1985. Jolly Jack's cabin sits on the left bank.
(Inset) Jolly Jack Thornton photographed in front of his cabin near the turn of the century.

Marcus, Washington, where he enjoyed success on Jolly Jack's Bar, so named in his honour, from which he and his partners recovered $20,084.

For years afterward he followed the will-o'-the-wisp, participating in every gold rush from Wild Horse Creek east to Granite Creek, and from Big Bend south into the state of Washington.

It was in Colville that Thornton met and married Louise Polly Busch, who for years worked side by side with her husband on his various claims. Eventually, the Thorntons returned to the Boundary Country where they built a house on the little flat of Boundary Creek very near where the ruins of his small cabin yet stands. There they raised a family of four girls and two boys — seven other children having died at birth. This house was later destroyed by fire and all traces of it have disappeared.

ORIGINAL LEGEND

John Thornton devoted 40 years of his life in search of golden wealth. That it eluded him is evidenced by the fact that Mrs. Thornton was forced to take in washing to help support the family. But fruitless years of hard labour did not seem to bother Thornton who, because of his congenial and cheerful attitude, was often referred to as "Jolly Jack."

But if Thornton was not a successful miner, he was certainly a persistent one, the record showing that at least until 1894, at age 70, he was still working a placer claim at the mouth of Norweigan Creek. Thornton prospected during the summers, and trapped in winter — a routine he followed for as long as he was able.

Then one day it happened. It was a spring evening when Thornton returned home from another mining expedition. Dumping a baking powder tin of coarse, copper-coloured nuggets on the table, Thornton announced to his wife that he had finally struck it big. Beyond that, however, he would not divulge any other information.

One of the old prospectors who saw the gold described it as "coarse and heavy, with nuggets up to an ounce. Most of it was bright, although much redder than placer gold usually is, the remainder was heavily oxidized, giving it a dark coppery tone."

Thornton was apparently a heavy drinker, and in the celebrations that followed in the Greenwood saloons, he was continually pressed about his discovery. But, drunk or sober, Thornton never gave the slightest hint where the nuggets came from. Said one old-timer in recent years: "You know, Thornton had a reputation for being talkative, and in many ways he was, but when the subject of his secret placer was brought up, he always clammed up. Nobody, not even his own family, ever found out where it was — he never dropped a hint."

When his nuggets ran out, Thornton and his horse Rosie headed out for a fresh supply. They always left for the claim early in the morning and always returned before nightfall. Thornton knew there were men who would kill for his secret, so he always made sure he was never followed. As a precaution, however, he was always fully armed.

How many trips Thornton made to his secret location is not recorded. Eventually, however, he became ill and could no longer make the journey. When his illness rendered him helpless, he was taken to the Old Men's Home in Kamloops, where, on April 3, 1903, he died. Right to the end, perhaps believing he would recover, Thornton would not confide the location of his placer even to his wife. Thus, the secret of the coarse, copper-coloured nuggets died with him.

Since Thornton's death, many individuals have searched in vain for his lost placer. Some, believing he may actually have cached nuggets around his cabin, have dug numerous holes in the area. No one, so far as is known, has ever found anything.

THE LOST PLACER — FOUND?

N.L. Barlee, a retired school teacher, noted historian and collector of gold rush memorabilia, first published the story of Jolly Jack and his lost placer in an 1974 issue of *Canada West*, an historical magazine he founded. Barlee had apparently been told the story by old prospectors who had seen the gold, describing it as "coarse and heavy, with nuggets up to an ounce. Most of it was bright, although much redder than placer gold usually is, the remainder was heavily oxidized, giving it a dark, coppery tone."

Barlee became convinced that the lost placer probably existed somewhere in the Boundary Country, but where? "Jack Thornton had lived and mined on Boundary Creek for years," wrote Barlee. "South of the falls it had been exceptionally rich in places, but that section of the creek was open and it would have been impossible for old Thornton, or anyone else, to have worked that stretch of the creek undetected. Besides, the character of the gold from Boundary Creek differed somewhat from the gold of the lost placer. That left only one area — Fourth of July Creek and its few branch streams. Little was actually known about the history of that region except that placer gold had been discovered there in 1859 by a band of American prospectors. Some coarse gold had been found but the creeks had a reputation for being spotty and it seemed unlikely that any of them — Fourth of July, May or little known Taylor — any one of which a person can step across in low water, would be logical locations. I knew that a number of prospectors had scoured the Boundary Country for years, searching for the elusive placer creek. Most of them had been experienced miners, and their sharp eyes seldom missed the tell-tale signs which indicated that a creek or area had been worked. But they too had come up empty-handed."

Barlee found the story perplexing and fascinating, but, having exhausted all leads, had almost forgotten about the lost placer

John "Jolly Jack" Thornton's crumbling log cabin on the bank of Boundary Creek a few miles west of Greenwood, in July 1985.

(Left) Spotting these rocks along a dirt road near Phoenix in 1985, the author stopped to investigate. Just over the hill was found the man-made mound cache shown above. Nearby lay the ruins of cabins.

(Below) These ruins were located a couple of miles beyond Phoenix and not far from Skeff Creek.

until he happened to stop in Greenwood some years later. While having coffee with an old friend named Peter den Hartog, or "Big Pete," the conversation drifted to gold mining. Suddenly, Peter rose from the table and left the room. When he returned he emptied the contents of a container before Barlee. "Half a pound of coarse gold and nuggets lay glittering in front of me," wrote Barlee.

Peter told Barlee that he thought he might have found Jolly Jack's lost placer. He went on to explain that he had found the gold on Skeff Creek, a little creek which used to be called Taylor Creek, that flowed into Fourth of July Creek just above May Creek.

Intrigued by the possibility that his friend may have actually discovered the lost placer, Barlee spent the next few weeks examining all the documentation he had about the lost mine. Among the pieces of information was a letter written by May Jones, one of Thornton's surviving daughters, in 1967. It stated:

"My mother told me that my father really had found something very rich, but where it was he took to the Great Beyond with him. Before he got too ill he took his horse Rosie. It was in the spring of the year. He left home in the morning and was back at night and he had a baking powder can full of nuggets when he came home. He was old and so was his horse so he could not have gone far. She said he told her that they had struck it rich at last, but he never told mother where it was, or anyone else. Many have looked for it but none have found the place yet."

Barlee gleaned two valuable clues from this letter. First, Thornton had made his trip in the spring. This was important because Skeff, an insignificant creek, "often dries up in summer or early fall. The only time it flows with a volume of water adequate for sluicing is in the spring. . . ." Second, Thornton and his aging horse had made the round trip in one day. Barlee examined a map of the Boundary Country. He was curious to see how far Skeff Creek was from Thornton's old cabin, the remains of which still litter Boundary Creek just west of Greenwood.

"The most logical route," Barlee determined, "was a seldom used trail which passed through the high country south of the old mining town of Phoenix, between Mt. Attwood and Deadman Hill. If he had taken that trail the distance between his cabin and Skeff Creek was only seven and a half miles." Thornton would have no difficulty covering that distance and returning by evening.

Barlee became intrigued enough by the possibility that he decided to make a personal survey of Skeff Creek; but when he arrived on the creek in early July he was not impressed. Of the hundreds of gold creeks he had visited over the years, none looked less promising.

"I gradually worked upstream," wrote Barlee, "looking for any indicators which might substantiate the lost placer theory. There were signs all along proving that miners had been at work in years past. The banks of the stream showed increasing evidence of placer operations as I moved upward. I passed by several abandoned sluice boxes, a broken rocker and the decaying remains of several ancient log cabins. Entering a narrow defile I noticed piles of tailings. 'Tailings' is a term used by placer miners to describe boulders which were removed to recover the gold lying on bedrock. The rocks had been painstakingly stacked on the banks of the creek so I knew that Chinese miners had once been there. White miners were invariably more slipshod than their Chinese counterparts, and they seldom piled their tailings as carefully. I was disappointed because I was aware that any creek the Chinese had mined was usually worked out. Although they sometimes missed paystreaks, it was not a common occurrence.

"Somewhat disheartened, I continued on up the draw and passed under a sagging wooden bridge. Just beyond the bridge I paused. The old Chinese workings had suddenly stopped. For some inexplicable reason the oriental miners had worked up the creek to that point, and then had simply quit. They had obviously abandoned the creek at that spot."

From Barlee's research, he knew of only a few reasons why the Chinese would abandon a placer creek; lack of gold, lack of water, or they had been driven off their ground by white miners.

"I knew they hadn't run out of gold because Big Pete and others before him had obtained both coarse gold and nuggets just a few yards farther up the creek, so that wasn't the reason. They could have run out of water in the dry season, but when a stream was worth working, and Skeff certainly was, they would have done their dead work in the dry months and then mined the creek in the spring when the water was high. I crossed off that reason too. And historically, the Chinese had not been driven off any of the placer creeks anywhere in the Boundary Country, so that wasn't the answer either. There had to be another explanation."

Then, as Barlee stood examining the rough terrain, the answer suddenly struck him. On both banks massive boulders, some of them 30 tons or more, loomed ominously. "One of the Chinese miners must have been killed undercutting one of the boulders," Barlee wrote. "Undercutting and propping boulders to get at the gold underneath them is one of the most dangerous jobs in mining, and although the Chinese were experts at it, they too occasionally made mistakes."

Barlee knew that the Chinese traditionally abandoned any creek where one of their countrymen had been killed, usually within hours. He also knew that others had mined the creek after the Chinese left. Old Cal Hopper had leased the ground and worked the creek for years. Before Hopper died in 1943, he always had several medicine bottles full of coarse gold in his cabin. After Hopper's death, "his lease passed into a succession of hands, none of whom was aware of its intriguing history. The coarse gold continued to turn up in tantalizing quantities but the boulders and overburden which had hampered former operations continued to plague them and, after tapping the creek for some of its riches, they gave up or moved on to easier ground elsewhere."

Skeff Creek lay nearly deserted for almost two decades until the lease was abandoned in 1972. Then it was acquired by Big Pete, who, for the next two summers, "systematically mined a small section of the ground and recovered ounce after ounce of gold."

As the summer passed, and Barlee dug deeper into the history of the area, he came to the conclusion that Jolly Jack's long sought placer was somewhere on Skeff Creek. Barlee concluded: "There is still gold on Skeff Creek — coppery hued and very coarse. It's more difficult to recover today, the overburden is deeper and the boulders still guard their hoard as they have for more than a century. But when the twenty, thirty and fifty dollar nuggets turn up and the gold lies glinting on the bedrock, the old mine always seems close at hand. And there is almost half a mile of ground along the creek which has never been touched by any miner. It's there, just up from the historic Dewdney Trail and south of that landmark known as Deadman Hill. Somewhere along that stretch, above the Chinese diggings, Jolly Jack's lost mine may still lie hidden, awaiting discovery."

SUMMARY AND CONCLUSION

In examining the major gold producing areas in the Boundary Country, the Rock Creek region was easily the most celebrated area. Rock Creek, and its tributaries like Jolly Jack, McKinney and Baker were all gold bearing. Thornton, in addition to his claim on Boundary Creek, also worked a claim on Rock Creek. According to a short article by Henry Nicholsen in the 1976 report of the *Boundary Historical Society:* "J. Thornton and his partner had some good ground about 12 miles up the creek, which paid them about $10 a day to the hand. . . ." Further confirmation appeared in the 1979 report, where F. Western Smith wrote that Thornton had a claim on ". . .Jolly Jack Creek, near Camp McKinney." Smith goes on to state: "There was a cabin and approximately 200 yards from it was a tunnel or adit, in the clay bank. It is told by oldtimers and grandchildren that he took $60,000 from this location."

The Rock Creek area would appear to be the most likely location of Thornton's secret placer, if it existed, except for one thing. Almost everyone agrees that the location had to be within easy riding distance from Thornton's cabin, since, according to legend, Thornton always made the round trip in one day. This would tend to be confirmed by the letter May Jones wrote in 1967, which was quoted earlier in this story. But how much credibility should be given to information supplied 64 years after Thornton's death?

Fortunately, unlike most treasure stories, a great deal is known about the life and death of John Thornton. Much of this information was written by E. Jacobs immediately following the funeral of Thornton and was printed in the May, 1903 issue of *The Mining Record*. The background on Thornton is quite detailed, yet at no time is there any suggestion of his having discovered a mysterious source of gold. In fact, the article paints quite a different picture of Thornton's financial situation.

We learn, for example, that in the latter years of his life, Thornton survived on a "periodical pension allowance from the United States Government." Between these "quarterly" remittances, it was the generosity of other old placer miners that helped Thornton get by, resulting "in some little creature comfort or other finding its way to the old man's cabin."

We also learn that John "had long lived alone, Mrs. Thornton and children having their home in another cabin a short distance away." For the years the Thornton's lived apart, Mrs. Thornton "took in daywork and washing to support the family," and after John's death there was great concern over the bringing up of the children.

This hardly looks like someone who had a limitless source of gold at his disposal. If, as the legend states, "When his nuggets ran out, Thornton and his horse Rosie headed out for a fresh supply," it is highly unlikely that he and his family would have lived under such poverty. So how did this legend start?

We know that Thornton did make at least two rich strikes; one on Jolly Jack's Bar, in Washington; the other on Rock Creek. There were probably others as well, for *The Mining Record* refers to him as being "At times flush and spending his hard-earned gold with all the recklessness of one who had an abundance from which to draw supplies, and again 'dead broke' and glad of a little timely assistance from others more fortunate for the time being."

What if, after Thornton's death, someone innocently suggested that he must have had a secret mine because he had spent his "hard-earned" gold as though he "had an abundance from which to draw supplies?" Over the prevailing years that innocent comment would become rumour, then fact, and finally, legend. Then, what if, upon questioning 64 years later, Thornton's daughter May confused the situation by stating that her mother had told her, "that father had really struck something very rich?" But, what if her mother had only been referring to one of his more successful claims?

Contrary to the legend, Thornton did not die at the Old Men's Home in Kamloops. "Jolly Jack died in his snug little 10x12 log cabin situate at the junction of Norwegian Creek with Boundary Creek, and on a placer claim the old man had held and worked for many years." While this information does not directly negate the possibility of a lost placer, it does illustrate how known facts can become distorted or forgotten over a period of years.

Thornton was in deteriorating health for quite some time before his death, and was being cared for by the Pioneer's Association of Okanagan and South Yale. During the summer of 1902, this association had arranged for Thornton to be admitted into the Old Men's Home at Kamloops. But it was not until October, 1902, that "the old fellow would consent to leave his cabin for the, to him, uncongenial surroundings of such an institution." But Thornton soon tired of life there, and during the winter he returned to his cabin on Boundary Creek. "Before going to his cabin he spent a couple of days with old friends at 'Billy' Nelson's Pioneer Hotel, Greenwood, and around the big stove in the cheery bar of that popular resort of old-timers, stories of long ago were dug up afresh, old-time ditties (including the old man's particular favourite, 'I'm Jolly Jack, the Rover,' which he sang in strong voice and with as much spirit as ever) were sung once again and the hours passed so pleasantly that the old fellow perked up, feeling, as he confided to his old friend 'Major' Charlie Collins, 'so good, and right glad to be back among the boys once more.' "

A month later Thornton's health had failed to the point that a man was sent to stay with and take care of him. During his last few days his memory failed him so badly that he could not recognize even his most intimate friends. But he knew his wife, and she stayed by his side until the end on Wednesday, April 1, 1903.

Thornton was well known and well liked, and his funeral, which took place on April 3, was well attended. John "Jolly Jack" Thornton was buried in a grave which ". . .had been dug in the 'wash' within a stone's throw from the cabin and near to where a small white-railed and picketed enclosure marked the place of burial of two infant children of the Thorntons."

Whether or not Thornton had ever tapped into the riches of Skeff Creek will never be known with any certainty. But if Skeff Creek did produce coarse nuggets, and indeed still does, it is certainly worth examining in its own right, regardless of any legend. As for Jolly Jack's lost placer, the known facts have been presented in this story; the final decision, however, is up to you.

9

THE LOST MORGAN MINE

*Gordon ran the assay on the specimens brought to
him by Morgan that night. They were staggeringly
rich, containing between 400 and 500 ounces of silver,
and from four to five ounces of gold, per ton.*

T HE earliest known mining operations in the Boundary
district were conducted in 1862 when portions of
Boundary Creek were worked for placer gold.
Between 1862 and 1891 little interest was taken by prospectors in
this district and few claims were staked. That changed in 1890,
when the discoveries of gold-copper ore bodies at Rossland
stimulated prospecting over extensive areas in southern British
Columbia. In 1891 prospecting was actively carried out in the
vicinity of Greenwood, at which time the Mother Lode, Crown
Silver, and Sunset were staked.

Strategically located at the junction of Boundary and Twin
creeks, Greenwood was the brainchild of Robert Wood. Only two
cabins had occupied the site of the future city in October, 1894,
when Wood bought the land from Otto Dillier, who had pre-empted
there the previous year. Gambling $5,000, Wood built a network
of roads to link his proposed town with much of the Boundary
Country. Little more than a year later, Greenwood consisted of
three stores, three hotels, a butcher shop, blacksmith, two livery
stables, two lawyers' offices, a newspaper, public hall, hospital and
school.

Greenwood officially became a city in August of 1897, and by
1899, the new city was in the pink of economic health. Its
population, which stood at 2,500, had doubled in just the last six
months. The advent of the railway-smelter era promised even
greater prosperity. By mid-February, 1900, Greenwood truly
entered the 20th century when a number of businesses and private
homes were illuminated by electric lights.

ORIGINAL LEGEND

His name was Harry Morgan and he was an American who had

Ruins of the Greenwood Smelter in 1884. (Inset) Canadian Pacific Railway locomotive #952 at the Mother Lode mine near Greenwood, 1903.

drifted in from Chewaw, Washington, a little stopping-place just across from Bridesville in the Boundary Country.

It was near the turn of the century when he hit Greenwood. In those years the "Boundless Boundary" was in the midst of a spectacular mining boom and all sorts of characters and promoters were in the area hoping to participate in the wealth. It looked like every available piece of ground, no matter how remote, had been investigated by prospectors and over 800 claims had been recorded; all the way from Camp McKinney in the west to Burnt Basin in the east.

Morgan sized up the situation and quickly concluded that all the good ground had been taken up but, as he was a trapper as well as a prospector, he decided that he would eke out a living by trapping until he could latch onto a good mineral claim. With this plan in mind he left Greenwood and headed north.

Following Boundary Creek, Morgan passed the silver-rich Providence Camp, and a few miles further on, Long Lake Camp, until he neared the headwaters of the creek. Finally, about 18 miles north of Greenwood, he stopped. It was a remote region and it looked, to his experienced eye, like good trapping country. Within a few days Morgan had erected a crude sod-roofed hut and had set out his traps.

Like so many other trappers and prospectors in the area, Morgan was seldom seen in town except when he was in purchasing supplies. Even then he attracted little attention because of his diminutive size and his unusual taciturnity; he was generally regarded as a strange man who had no known close friends.

Several years passed with Morgan's usual twice-a-year trips being his only contact with Greenwood. One fall, however, he deviated from his general pattern and turned up in Greenwood again just several days after he had left town. This time, instead of heading for a general merchant's store, Morgan went to an assayer, a certain Captain Gordon. Gordon, one of numerous assayers in the district, had a reputation for being very close-mouthed. This was probably the reason Morgan chose him in preference to several others.

Upon arriving at the assayer's place, Morgan untied two sacks which had been tied to his black pony, and with some difficulty succeeded in packing them into the assayer's office. Once inside he tersely asked Gordon to assay the ore. Gordon, who had never seen Morgan before, took the sacks from the prospector and spilled the contents out onto the table. He heft a piece of the ore and noted that it was very heavy. His shrewd eye also perceived that the samples were chunky and had obviously come from a vein of considerable width, not a narrow deposit.

Nonchalantly, Captain Gordon agreed to run an assay on it to see what values, if any, it contained. Morgan looked warily at him and mumbled that he would return in a few days to find out the results. A moment later he was gone.

Gordon ran the assay that very night and was dumbfounded to learn that the ore contained between 400 and 500 ounces of silver, and from five to six ounces of gold to the ton — it was staggeringly rich.

A few days later the prospector returned and listened impassively as the excited assayer read out the assay results. After Gordon finished he cautioned Morgan that if he had not staked the ground yet, he had better do so in a big hurry. The prospector shook his head negatively and stated that nobody else would ever find his mine anyway.

According to local reports, Morgan returned to Greenwood every few months with more samples for assaying and the results were always the same; extremely high values in silver and gold.

Finally, after several years association with the old prospector, the assayer gained Morgan's confidence and was eventually invited to go out and take a look at the mine. He readily consented and a date and time was set. On that day Gordon left Greenwood and proceeded up Boundary Creek where he was to meet with Morgan at a pre-designated spot several miles south of the headwaters region. After travelling most of the day he arrived at the place agreed upon and found the old man waiting there. They set off together for the headwaters but, as the assayer later related, the prospector seemed to display signs of nervousness the farther up the creek they travelled until finally, in Gordon's words, "He just took off through the jack pines." And from that day on Captain Gordon never saw Morgan again, he simply vanished.

The disappointed assayer made his way back to Greenwood and waited vainly for several weeks for the old prospector to turn up. Finally, possessed with curiosity, Gordon travelled into the area again to search for the old prospector. Although Gordon was successful in locating Morgan's sod-roofed cabin, there was no sign of the prospector or the mine which had produced the fabulous silver ore. Keenly disappointed, he returned to town and related the details to several close friends. One look at the ore convinced most doubters, and in the following months a number of other prospectors made efforts to locate "Morgan's Mine," but to no avail. Morgan had disappeared and his mine could not be found.

Some individuals made concentrated efforts to locate it. One old hand from Deadwood, Scott McRae, established a trapline in the area and spent years searching for it but drew a blank. Another trapper, Vic Barrett, set up his trapline in the same region after McRae had gone. Barrett was the complete woodsman, strong as a horse and well versed in every aspect of woods lore. Barrett, however, was more fortunate than his predecessor for he finally succeeded in finding one important clue — Morgan's wheelbarrow, a crude affair which the old prospector had used to truck the silver ore out of his mine. The wheelbarrow had been found on a ridge about one and a half miles from the headwaters. Sensing that he was finally hot on the trail, Barrett scoured the immediate area but was unable to find any sign of the mine. He finally gave up after days of searching and concluded that the wily Morgan had carefully camouflaged the entrance to the mine to prevent anyone else from finding it.

In later years Barrett led numerous expeditions into the area in search of the Morgan Mine but they were always unsuccessful. He continued into his late seventies and even up until his death in Greenwood on April 23, 1962, at 86 years of age, he was convinced that it was still near the headwaters of Boundary Creek awaiting rediscovery.

There were others who were equally certain. One was Fritz Hauzner who had a ranch up Boundary Creek. Hauzner had evidently procured some of the ore from Gordon, the assayer. It was phenomenally rich and bore out the first assays of the ore.

SUMMARY AND CONCLUSION

The known facts are interesting. The formation near the headwaters of Boundary Creek is primarily granite-diorite, but the Boundary Country, although noted for its copper producers, has had many celebrated silver mines. Some, like the Providence, Elkhorn, Skylark and Last Chance produced millions of dollars in silver ore in their day. Since the Lost Morgan Mine is suppose to be in the vicinity of the Providence, lets concentrate on mines in that immediate area.

The first mention of the Providence mine in the *Minister of Mines* report comes in 1893: "On the Providence mine, situated about five miles up the (Boundary) creek from the American Boy, one shaft is down 70 feet, and a second shaft 15 feet, from which, since June last, 500 sacks of ore, together weighing 32,500 lbs., have been sent to the Tacoma smelter, giving an average return of *400 ozs. in silver and one ounce in gold per ton.* (Emphasis mine.) The Defiance claim, adjacent to the Providence, which was recorded on the 4th of September last, has a shaft down 20 feet, from which 67 sacks or ore, weighing about 4,350 lbs., have also been sent to the smelter at Tacoma, and yielded *560 ozs. in silver, and two ozs. in gold per ton.* (Emphasis mine.) The Skylark mine, situate about three miles easterly from the Providence camp. . .was recorded on the 28th of July last, since which time two shafts have been sunk on the claim, one 55 feet and the other 15 feet, from which 425 sacks of ore, weighing 27,625 lbs., were sent to the smelter at Tacoma, and yielded *268 ozs. in silver and one ounce in gold per ton.* " (Emphasis is again mine.)

This information clearly illustrates that the area in which the Lost Morgan Mine is supposed to be located was extremely rich in silver ore. In fact, the assay report of Morgan's specimens of

A general view of Greenwood's downtown commercial centre c1900, with Boundary Creek on the left. The bridge led to the Greenwood smelter.

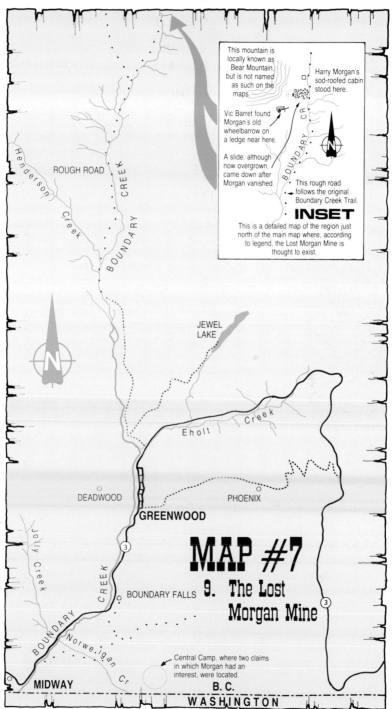

This mountain is locally known as Bear Mountain, but is not named as such on the maps.

Harry Morgan's sod-roofed cabin stood here.

Vic Barret found Morgan's old wheelbarrow on a ledge near here.

A slide, although now overgrown, came down after Morgan vanished.

This rough road follows the original Boundary Creek Trail.

INSET

This is a detailed map of the region just north of the main map where, according to legend, the Lost Morgan Mine is thought to exist.

ROUGH ROAD

Henderson Creek

BOUNDARY CREEK

JEWEL LAKE

Eholt Creek

DEADWOOD

PHOENIX

GREENWOOD

Jolly Creek

BOUNDARY CREEK

BOUNDARY FALLS

Norwegian Cr.

MAP #7

9. The Lost Morgan Mine

Central Camp, where two claims in which Morgan had an interest, were located.

MIDWAY   **B. C.**

WASHINGTON

"between 400 and 500 ounces of silver, and from five to six ounces of gold to the ton" are certainly in line with the known yields of the three mines emphasized in italics above. This confirms, therefore, that the existence of a rich silver mine in this area "would be" possible.

As for the principal character, Harry Morgan, we know that he did exist. Unfortunately, the 1907 *Minister of Mines* report is the only one which contains any reference to a Harry Morgan in the Greenwood district, and that is extremely sketchy. He is listed, in partnership with Duncan McIntosh, William. M. Law, Frank J. Miller and Patrick Hickey as the owners of two claims in the area. The Little Ruth, consisting of 12.63 acres, was located on lot 881.S, while the No. 9, consisting of 13.65 acres, was on the adjoining lot 882.S. Both claims were granted on November 25, 1907. Although Morgan's middle initial is listed as "K" on the Little Ruth claim and "L" on the No. 9 claim, there can be no doubt that they are one and the same. Is this, however, the Harry Morgan of legend?

According to the original legend, Morgan first came to Greenwood "near the turn of the century," or around 1900. Later we learn that "several years passed" before Morgan made his discovery. According to the dictionary, "several" means "more than two." This would place the discovery at 1903 at the earliest. Still later we learn that it was only after "several years association" with assayer Gordon that Morgan decided to take him to him mine. That date can be no earlier than 1906. Since the Morgan claims were recorded on November 25, 1907, I think it is safe to assume that the Harry Morgan listed in the mining report and the Harry Morgan of the legend are one and the same. With that established, lets examine his two known claims.

Unfortunately, the *Minister of Mines* makes no further mention of the Little Ruth. The No. 9, however, does have a history dating back to 1897 when it was owned by S.S. Fowler. His claim was either permitted to lapse or he sold it to the Morgan group. In any event, the No. 9 was located in the "Central Camp," and consisted of ores which were "gold or silver-bearing veins." Since the Little Ruth was located on the lot next to No. 9, it would also have been located in the Central Camp area. Where then, was the Central Camp?

Referring again to the 1897 report, we find that "Central Camp, locally known as White's, Douglas and Attwood's Camps, lie at an elevation of 4,000 to 4,500 feet along the very heavily timbered mountain spur at the head of Douglas Creek, 8 miles by trail from Midway, and five miles from Boundary Falls."

Unfortunately, none of the mining reports indicate in which direction Central Camp is located in relation to Midway or Boundary Falls. However, by placing an eight mile circumference around Midway and a five mile circumference around Boundary

Falls, I found that they intersected in only two places. The first is eight miles north-northeast of Midway and five miles northwest of Boundary Falls. The second is eight miles due east of Midway and five miles south-southeast of Boundary Falls.

The reference to Douglas Creek was another puzzle, there being no such creek on modern maps. However, further research led me to a rough, hand-drawn map of the Boundary Country in the book *Border Gold.* According to this map, Douglas Creek enters Boundary Creek directly opposite from Jolly Creek. On modern maps, this creek is now called Norweigan. Central Camp is shown at the head of this creek, which, incidentally, matches exactly our second intersecting circumference site.

Finding the location of Central Camp has, however, caused some problems with the Lost Morgan Mine theory. As can be seen on the accompanying map, Morgan's known claims are nowhere near the headwaters of Boundary Creek, north of Greenwood, where his lost mine is said to exist. Quite the contrary, the Morgan claims are located 10 miles due south of Greenwood. While this information does not in itself disprove the existence of the Lost Morgan Mine, it does create some rather obvious holes in the legend, and must give one pause for thought.

On the positive side, we know that Morgan existed and that he was in the Greenwood area at least until 1907. We know also that the lost mine's "supposed" location, north of Greenwood, was known to produce rich silver ore. The original legend also claims that Morgan had a cabin at the headwaters of Boundary Creek, and that his wheelbarrow was found in the area by Vic Barrett and seen by a number of locals. However, since there is no documentation to verify that the cabin or wheelbarrow actually belonged to Morgan, this cannot be substantiated as fact. Neither, however, can it be determined to be false.

This information must be tempered by the fact that Morgan's known claims were located 10 miles due south of Greenwood, not north. These claims were obviously not very worthwhile or they would have been given more ink in the mining reports. Since no information is published about them, we can assume that they were abandoned after some exploratory work was done. Still, if Morgan took the trouble to stake these claims, does it not stand to reason that if he had found a rich claim elsewhere he would have registered it as well?

Where Morgan went or what happened to him is highly debatable. Some suggest he might have been killed in a cave-in at his mine or pack-trained some ore across the line and then decided not to return. It would appear more likely, however, at least in the absence of further information, that he simply moved on to other areas and was not heard from again.

His lost mine, however, may live on forever. And who knowns,

(Above) The Greenwood Inn (originally Windsor Hotel, 1896) on Green-wood's Copper Street in October, 1984. The Traveler's Cafe was originally the Pacific Hotel which opened for business in 1896.
(Below) Greenwood City Hall.

perhaps one day information will come forth that will prove or disprove, once and for all, its existence. Until then, one can always dream.

10

THE LOST LEMON MINE

After discovering gold, partners Blackjack and Lemon became embroiled in a bitter argument; an argument that was settled later that night when Lemon seized the camp axe and murdered his sleeping companion.

SOMEWHERE in the rocky foothills of the Highwood Mountain Range lies the secret of Alberta's greatest lost treasure. The fabulous Lost Lemon Mine, according to legend, has defied searchers for over a century, and supposedly lured many men to their deaths.

As is the case with most lost mines, however, it is all but impossible to sift fact from fiction. This task is made even more difficult by the numerous stories which have appeared on the Lost Lemon over the years. One poorly researched version even placed the lost mine in British Columbia.

On the other hand, the best and most authoritative account was rendered by the late Senator Daniel Riley, Tom Primrose and Hugh Dempsey in the Frontier book entitled *The Lost Lemon Mine — The Greatest Mystery of the Canadian Rockies.*

The story of the Lost Lemon Mine seems to have appeared for the first time in a 1946 issue of the *Alberta Folklore Quarterly.* Its author, Daniel Edward Riley, was born in Prince Edward Island and moved to the High River district of Alberta in 1882. Elected as mayor of High River in 1906, he was eventually elected to the Senate in 1925. Riley died two years after his article, which has caused a sensation ever since, first appeared in print.

ORIGINAL LEGEND

According to Riley, the story began at Tobacco Plains, Montana, in the spring of 1870. Tobacco Plains is an area about 20 miles by 30 miles, two-thirds of which lies in British Columbia. It was from the Montana side that a prospecting party numbering 35 to 40 men gathered for a trip to the North Saskatchewan River, after hearing rumours of gold discoveries in the area. Two members of the group, known only as Blackjack and Lemon, would be immortalized for the rich strike they would make. Their prospecting venture had been staked by an old Indian trader known as Lafayette French.

Venturing northward, the party soon reached their destination, and the prospectors eagerly panned every stream and creek. Their efforts failed to show promising "color," however, and, discouraged, the expedition started back.

But, for Blackjack and Lemon, the search for the elusive yellow metal was just beginning. Abandoning the main party, and guided by a large band of half-breeds under La Nouse — for protection against the Blackfoot — they travelled south. Eventually, the two prospectors separated from this party also, electing to proceed on their own.

Finding an old Indian lodge-pole trail, they followed it up High River towards Tobacco Plains. Their travels led them along peaceful green valleys rimmed by rugged mountains, where cool streams knifed through lush forests abounding with game — a scene virtually unaltered to this day.

It was along one of these swift-flowing streams that the two prospectors first found traces of gold. Encouraged, they began exploring upstream and were eventually rewarded by the discovery of "rich diggings from grass roots to bedrock." Oddly enough, the gold had been discovered quite by chance, while bringing the horses in from the picket lines.

Once the exaltation of discovery had subsided, however, the two partners could not agree on whether to return to stake their claim or stay and work the diggings. This caused a heated argument that was effectively settled later that night when Lemon seized the camp axe and murdered his sleeping partner.

Suddenly gripped by the horror of his deed, Lemon would have fled the scene immediately, had it not been nightfall. To lessen his gathering panic, he built a large fire and spent the remainder of the night pacing nervously before it, gun beneath his arm, "like a caged wild beast."

Unknown to Lemon, his heinous crime had been witnessed by two Stoney Indian braves, William and Daniel Bendow. The whistles, shrieks and groans they emitted throughout the night nearly drove Lemon crazy, and in fact may have been a contributing factor to his later insanity. Finally, with the first rays of sunlight, the tormented and demented killer mounted his horse and rode off.

Upon his departure, the two Indians ransacked the camp, pillaging supplies and the two abandoned horses, then returned to the Morley Reserve where they related the night's events to Chief Bearspaw. Fearing that gold-hungry miners would invade their hunting grounds, Bearspaw swore the brothers to secrecy — and the mine's location remains a secret to this day.

When Lemon reached Tobacco Plains, he revealed his crime to a priest, supposedly an old friend, with whom he spent the winter.

As evidence of his story, he produced the gold "they had discovered, but he seemed half-crazed from the recollections of his crime."

Nevertheless, the priest immediately dispatched John McDougall, a half-breed mountaineer, to the murder scene. Guided by Lemon's directions, he located the spot without difficulty, buried Blackjack, and "reared a mound of stones over the grave to keep off prowling wolves, and returned to Tobacco Plains." As soon as he left, however, Stoney Indians scattered the stones and obliterated all traces of the former campsite. Their work has proved effective, for the site has yet to be rediscovered!

By spring Lemon had regained a certain degree of sanity lost by the burden of his crime, and he agreed to lead a group of prospectors to the mine — having no doubts that he could locate it without difficulty.

However, although Lemon scoured the gullies and hillsides, he was unable to locate the site, and was accused by the angry miners of having deliberately misled them. Unable to cope with their accusations and threats of death, Lemon became violently mad, and had to be guarded constantly.

The following year the priest outfitted another party, this time under the guidance of the veteran mountaineer John McDougall, who had found the camp site and buried Blackjack the year before. McDougall, then at Fort Benton, was to join the party at Crowsnest Lake, and they would proceed north together from there. McDougall left Fort Benton as scheduled, but at Fort Kipp, a notorious whiskey-post, he drank himself to death. The search had to be abandoned.

The following year another attempt had to be aborted because of raging forest fires.

Undeterred, the priest outfitted yet another expedition the following year, once again headed by Lemon, who seemed to have recovered. This time Lemon found the general vicinity without much difficulty, but as he neared the murder scene, he became unbalanced once again.

Finally defeated, the priest abandoned his quest for the lost mine — but it was immediately taken up by others. However, although numerous attempts were made to locate it, none were as concentrated or determined as the efforts of one Lafayette French.

His first attempt to locate the mine was thwarted when he was suddenly stricken by a mysterious illness. French barely managed to drag himself back to Tobacco Plains, more dead than alive. Senator Riley, who staked French on some of his ventures, hinted that the sickness might be attributed to a curse of "voodoo."

Armed with a rough pen and ink map supposedly drawn by Lemon himself, French devoted the next 15 years of his life to the search, surrendering his savings and eventually his life in the process. While the map's existence is questionable, French's dedication to his self-imposed task was not.

French realized that his greatest hope of finding the lost mine hinged on William Bendow, one of the Indians who had witnessed the axe slaying. To gain his confidence, French fed and housed Bendow and his followers at his ranch one winter and offered Bendow 25 horses and 25 head of cattle if he would reveal the location. Bendow finally agreed, and the expedition eagerly started out. But on the second day, Bendow had a change of heart — either from the fear of superstition, or the fear of Chief Bearspaw himself — and refused to go another step.

Undaunted by this initial setback, French continued to concentrate his efforts on the Stoney brave, and eventually Bendow agreed to lead a second expedition. But, that night, Bendow died suddenly and mysteriously. His followers placed his body in a Red River cart and returned it fearfully to the Morley Reserve. When Bendow's son-in-law died on the night of their arrival in the same mysterious manner, the Indians were convinced that Bendow had suffered the wrath of Wahcondah for his intention to reveal the mine's location.

Still French persisted, scanning river and stream in his fruitless search. It was early in the winter of 1912 when French, staked by Senator Riley, had set out on yet another search for the mine. He was returning home from a field trip one evening when he came across an old log cabin at a place known as Emerson's Crossing. It was late, so he decided to stay there for the night.

Later that night the cabin was mysteriously engulfed in flames. That French escaped at all was a miracle, but he was so badly burned that he had to crawl most of the way to the Beddingfield Ranch, some two miles away. The ordeal took several hours, and by the time he reached the bunkhouse, the men were all out working.

Exhausted, French dragged himself into one of the bunks and passed out. His presence was not detected until after supper that evening, at which point he was rushed to the hospital at High River. French immediately summoned Dan Riley, and managed to utter, "I know all about the Lost Lemon Mine now," before the doctor made him rest. As much as Riley wanted to know the details, he was forced to wait until morning. Unfortunately, French died in the night without regaining consciousness, taking his secret to the grave with him.

SUMMARY AND CONCLUSION

To lend credence to any lost treasure, it is imperative to authenticate as many of the characters and facts as possible. In this regard, very little was revealed by Riley about the two principal characters, Blackjack and Lemon. However, Riley provided one

A reproduction of a full colour painting depicting the murder scene as Lemon is about to slay his sleeping companion with an axe.

vital clue when he wrote that "Blackjack had the reputation of being the best prospector in the West since he was the real discoverer of the Cariboo diggings in British Columbia." Using that clue, Glenbow archivist Hugh Dempsey was able to track down a well-known Cariboo prospector named Nehemia T. Smith. Nicknamed Blackjack, "he joined the Fraser River gold rush in 1858 and there started a long partnership with Thomas Latham, also known as 'Dancing Bill.' He went to the Cariboo in the following year and made several fortunes, his most famous being the Blackjack tunnel on William's Creek in 1862." Unfortunately, although Smith appears to be the Blackjack of legend, he was sick but still alive in a Victoria hospital in 1883, 13 years after he was supposedly murdered by Lemon.

Gold prospectors were a wandering breed, always chasing the elusive rainbow. Thus, when the Cariboo gold rush began to wane, many prospectors headed north to the Ominica and Cassiar. Cassiar Gold Commissioner J.H. Sulliven, in the 1875 *Minister of Mines* report, might therefore have listed another candidate for the Blackjack of legend when he wrote: "A party of prospectors consisting of Mr. Neil McArthur, M.J. Smith, alias 'Black Jack,' and two others. . .have left McDame's Creek with the intention of proceeding some 70 miles in a northerly direction to prospect the tributaries of Detour River." Although this is once again long after the Blackjack of our legend was killed, it does serve to illustrate that "Blackjack" was a rather common nickname.

Tracking the elusive Mr. Lemon was even more challenging. Although he has been given the first name of Joe, Mark or Bill, none of the many versions of the treasure story that have appeared provided any clues to him whatsoever. Happily, I was successful in tracking down two fascinating leads. The first appeared in L.V. Kelly's *The Range Men* which was first published around 1913.

"A man named Mark Lemon, at present living in Montana, tells of a prospecting trip he and a party made into the Porcupine Hills in 1869. They found, he declares, placer gold of such exceeding richness that even their hopes were satisfied, but the Blackfeet or Peigans came down and killed all but Lemon, who upon escaping, has never returned, though he still asserts he knows the point where the placer deposits can be found. But though the Indian portion of this story might be true it is improbable that the gold part is, for every foot of the hills has been prospected again and again. No gold has ever been found there, though hundreds of men have panned the hillsides and streams. And yet some of the Peigans say they know where rich workings can be found."

The second was written by Sir Cecil Denny while he was archivist for the Alberta government from 1922-27. Reprinted in the 1958 *Alberta Historical Review,* Denny's account of Mark Lemon's encounter with the Blackfoot parallels that of Kelly's almost exactly, but Denny goes on to add:

"Another curious circumstance regarding gold in the Porcupine Hills is an occurrence that took place at Fort Macleod in 1875 and to which I was an eye witness. The firm of I.G. Baker & Co. furnished all supplies to the Mounted Police including beef. To furnish the beef needed, a herd of cattle belonging to that firm was allowed to graze in the Porcupine Hills west of Fort Macleod. A cow was driven down on one occasion for slaughter and on cutting open the paunch, considerable coarse gold and black sand was found in it. No fraud could be possible in the case as there was no reason in those days to start a gold rush and there were several men engaged in cutting up the animal who saw the gold taken from the paunch. Charles Conrad, at that time in charge of the store at Fort Macleod, had the gold on a plate on exhibition in his window for a long time. It was if I remember rightly, valued at about $60."

So we now have two fascinating accounts pertaining to a Mark Lemon and placer gold he had discovered. However, his reported discoveries were in the Porcupine Hills west of Fort MacLeod, not in the Highwood Range. Is this discovery the basis around which the Lost Lemon Mine legend has grown? Subsequent research tends to support that conclusion.

Two more individuals play important roles in our story, Lafayette French and a mysterious treasure-hunting priest. There is no disputing the existence of French, who was born in Pennsylvania and came to Alberta in the 1880s. Again referring to *The Range Men:* "French was an independent trader and consequently was not popular with the I.G. Baker Company. Though he doubtless took advantage of the Indians he probably did not do any worse than the others would. French's hold with the tribe (Blackfoot) dated from the time some years before when he saved Crowfoot's life on the High River."

Did French locate the Lost Lemon Mine? What did he mean when he supposedly stated in a letter that he had discovered it? When he told Dan Riley that he knew all about the Lost Lemon Mine, did he mean he had found the elusive mine, or that he had learned that it did not exist? These questions will never be answered with certainty.

Several years after French's death, rich gold-bearing ore was found in the ruins of the burnt cabin. It was believed to be associated with French and the Lost Lemon, but it had actually been smuggled into the country and planted there. A miner from Montana had salted the cabin, then pretended to discover gold so he could sell his stolen ore without suspicion.

Much controversy has developed over the identity of the priest, identified variously as Le Roux, LeRue or L'Hereux. The St. Ignatius Mission, south of Flathead Lake in Montana, served as the religious centre for Tobacco Plains. Jesuit records "do not acknowledge a

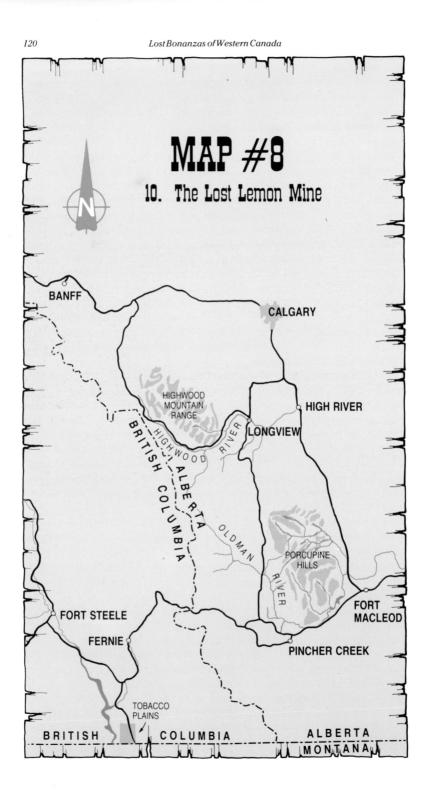

MAP #8

10. The Lost Lemon Mine

BANFF

CALGARY

HIGHWOOD
MOUNTAIN
RANGE

HIGH RIVER

HIGHWOOD   RIVER   LONGVIEW

BRITISH   ALBERTA

COLUMBIA

OLDMAN

RIVER

PORCUPINE
HILLS

FORT STEELE

FORT
MACLEOD

FERNIE

PINCHER CREEK

TOBACCO
PLAINS

BRITISH   COLUMBIA   ALBERTA

MONTANA

(Above) A view down a branch of the Highwood River, Alberta in 1884. It is
somewhere in this area that the Lost Lemon mine is supposedly lost.
(Below) Fort Benton in the early 1870s had become a bustling frontier town,
the gateway to the sprawling Northwest.

Placer operations at Wild Horse Creek, near Fort Steele, B.C.

priest, bogus or otherwise," at the Mission whose name even resembles those above. However, a man named Jean L'Heureux was well known among the Blackfoot as a "pretended priest." According to the Summer 1961 *Alberta Historical Review:* "Jean L'Heureux was born in Quebec and studied for the priesthood but was never ordained. He came west in about 1860 and passed himself off as a priest to the Jesuits in Montana. When he was exposed he joined the Blackfoot and in 1862 went to the Oblates at St. Albert where he convinced them that he was a priest. When the truth was discovered, he returned to the Blackfoot and remained among them, performing marriages, baptisms, etc. He was present at Treaty No. Seven in 1877 and served as interpreter for the Indian Department from 1879 to 1891. He then became a recluse near Pincher Creek and died in the Lacombe Home in 1919." Therefore, it seems likely that Jean L'Heureux was the priest in the legend.

Now, unfortunately, I must offer the most damaging piece of evidence against the existence of the Lost Lemon Mine. The story first appeared in the August 6, 1870 issue of the Helena *Daily Herald,* which appears undeniably to be the original source around which the entire Lost Lemon Mine legend has grown.

According to this article, an American prospector named "Frank Lemmon" claimed that in 1868 he and his partner "Old George" were with a party of 30 to 40 prospectors near Fort Edmonton. Upon encountering another party heading south, Lemmon and Old George decided to return with them. When they reached the vicinity of the present town of Nanton, however, Lemmon and Old George turned westward, hoping to find a pass which would lead them to the goldfields of Wild Horse Creek near Fort Steele.

The two men found a pass and later reached a creek on the west side of the Rocky Mountains (in British Columbia?) where they discovered gold in a gulch. It was after this discovery, according to Lemmon, that his "partner was killed by Indians about eighteen miles from the diggings. . .shot by the Blackfeet."

Lemmon eventually reached Helena where he tried unsuccessfully to interest other prospectors in returning with him, despite his claims of having recovered as much as "$15 or $20 to the pan in a gulch."

In the spring of 1870 Lemmon moved to a mining camp on Cedar Creek in Missoula where, after describing his gold-laden gulch, he succeeded in organizing a party headed under a man named Barnum. After travelling some 200 miles, Lemmon began to point out landmarks familiar to him, stating that the gulch was nearby. However, after several days of fruitless searching through rough terrain, Lemmon got lost. For a time the men prospected along the Flathead River, but, after their campfire raged out of control and destroyed nearly all their provisions, they gave up and returned to Cedar Creek.

There can be little doubt that the gold discovery of Frank Lemmon and Old George has served as the small seed from which an enormous legend has grown. The similarities are obvious, and keep in mind that this article was written within months of having actually happened. Likewise, there are many striking differences. Lemmon's partner was named Old George, not Blackjack, and, according to Lemmon, he was killed by Indians, although Lemmon would likely not have admitted to murdering his partner, if he had done so. These, and all other discrepancies, are probably the results of verbal telling and retelling, active imaginations and pure fabrications.

But the search for the lost mine, actually a lost placer, will undoubtedly continue. Senator Riley believes it has claimed more lives than Blackjack, Lemon and French. "There is a story of a white man's skeleton found in a gap of the Old Man river," he wrote, "the bony fingers still clutching a bag of gold. There is the story of two men, both badly wounded, stopping overnight in the 90s at a ranch in the foothills. They carried gold dust and were fleeing from the West. They rode away next morning for Fort MacLeod, but never arrived. Had they rediscovered the Lost Lemon Mine, only to be followed and killed by Indians?"

Today the legend continues, and men still venture into the Rocky Mountain foothills, certain the gold is there, that the Lost Lemon Mine really exists. Who knows for sure? Someday, someone may prove that it does.

11

GOLD FROM THE B.X. STAGE

*A treasure of $15,000 in gold nuggets and bars, the
results of an 1890 stagecoach robbery, is reputed
to be buried somewhere along Scottie Creek,
a few miles northeast of Cache Creek.*

THE discovery of gold in the Fraser River in 1858 led to the tumultuous gold rush that set New Caledonia (as British Columbia was then called) on its feet and assured it of its growth. The first means of conveyance into the region was by canoe over the network of waterways and lakes that blessed this new land. In the beginning, many hopeful prospectors surrendered their lives battling the raging Fraser that led to the heart of the goldfields. Soon trails were blazed through the virgin forests and ice-capped mountain peaks. Then, as mining camps began to prosper and grow, these pathways were widened to allow the passage of wagons.

The great inrush of miners from California naturally brought the expresses which were such a factor there. Wells, Fargo & Co. and their competitor Freeman & Co. both promptly opened offices in Victoria in 1858. Wells, Fargo & Co. did not themselves operate express lines in B.C., but in association with them Kent & Smith's Fraser and Thompson River Express operated on the lower Fraser River and on the Thompson River as far as Kamloops; and Lindhart & Bernard operated over the Douglas-Lillooet Trail.

Freeman & Co. connected at Victoria with Ballou's Pioneer Fraser River Express, established in June, 1858. It operated to the diggings via the Fraser River Canyon until 1859, when Wells, Fargo & Co. took over Freeman & Co. Ballou then connected with Wells, Fargo, and about that time he seems to have absorbed Lindhart & Bernard, as he then operated by both the Fraser Canyon and the Douglas-Lillooet routes to the interior.

In 1859, Jeffray's Fraser River Express started, by absorbing Kent & Smith's Express, and operated until December 1861, when it sold out to Barnard's Express, which was started in the autumn of

(Above) Barnard's Express office at Fort Yale with a stagecoach about to leave for points north.

(Left) Francis Jones Barnard, founder of the famous B.X. Express.

(Below) One Hundred Mile House on the Cariboo Road in 1868. It was from this yard that William Parker led the stagecoach shortly before the robbery.

1860. In 1861 the principal diggings moved 350 miles northward with a rush to the Cariboo district, with Ballou and Barnard competing.

In July, 1862, Barnard began to transport the mail on a semimonthly summer schedule; monthly during the winter. That October, Ballou, who had been not only the pioneer expressman in B.C., but had also been the first of the California operators in 1849, sold out to Dietz & Nelson, who in turn sold out to Barnard's in 1867.

During the years 1867-71 Barnard's B.C. Express held undisputed control of the mail and express service throughout the mainland of B.C. In 1871 Barnard unsuccessfully attempted to operate road steamers on the Cariboo Road instead of his four- and six-horse stages, and so lost the mail contract by being forced to bid too high. Gerow & Johnson's B.C. Express secured the mail contract that year, but they lasted only 10 months before selling out to Barnard.

In 1872 Barnard's Express was incorporated as F.J. Barnard & Co., and continued until 1879 when Barnard retired and the name was changed to the British Columbia Express Co. The famous horse stages to the Cariboo, commonly called "The B.X." continued to run until 1913, when motors were put on under a new company.

Along with passengers, freight and mail, the B.X. stage also transported valuable cargoes of gold from the Cariboo goldfields. For a time armed guards accompanied the shipments, but for many years the driver was the only guard. The B.X. moved vast quantities of the precious metal in their colourful red and yellow coaches, with $4,619,000 transported in 1865 alone. Yet, despite the great wealth carried by the stage, and the lack of an armed guard, very few robberies occurred. There were a few, however, and it is with the largest of these that we concern ourselves today.

ORIGINAL LEGEND

Our story begins one hot afternoon in July 1890, as a B.X. Stage was tortuously making its way up a steep grade near Bridge Creek. The six-horse stage had just clattered out of the dusty yard of 100 Mile House on its way south to Yale. In the red and yellow coach sat a travelling hide-buyer, the sole passenger. Also on board, beneath the driver's seat, was a strongbox containing $15,000 in nuggets and bars. The gold was on its way south to Yale for shipment to New Westminster by boat.

The stage driver was Steve Tingley, whose shouts and snapping whips urged the team onward. Lathering heavily, they pulled the creaking coach forward. Where the road widened somewhat, it was customary for the driver to pull the wheezing team to the roadside to cool off after their gruelling climb. Tingley had just set the handbrake and tied the reins, and was quietly enjoying the scenery of the sage-covered countryside, when a voice startled him.

"Throw up your hands, if you value your life," it ordered, and the distinctive cocking of a rifle confirmed it meant business.

Tingley complied without hesitation, then carefully turned around to see a man wearing a plaid shirt and slouch hat emerge from the bushes. His face was completely masked with a red bandana in which two eyeholes had been cut. In his hands, levelled at Tingley's head, was a Winchester.

"Toss down the box and be quick about it," ordered the bandit. "Don't try no funny stuff or I'll blow yer head off."

Realizing the hopelessness of the situation Tingley did as the highwayman commanded and threw the heavy box over the side. "Now move those horses and keep 'em movin'," warned the robber.

As the stage pulled away Tingley noticed that the robber was having problems with the strongbox, which was 18" square and built without handles to make a robber's task more difficult. Unable to cart off the heavy box, the bandit dragged it into the nearby bushes.

A former stage driver, Joe Burr, was in charge of the Provincial Police detachment in Ashcroft when word of the robbery reached him. A posse was hastily formed and set off in pursuit of the robber. They found the smashed, empty strongbox in the bushes where the thief had left it, but a thunderstorm had washed away any tracks he might have left.

The posse scoured the hills and surrounding region for the thief, and all suspicious characters were questioned. It was considered impossible for a robber to leave the rugged, isolated Cariboo country without being discovered, but, as the weeks passed, it was generally assumed that the robber had somehow eluded the law and made good his escape. There was not a trace of him anywhere. Gradually the excitement of the robbery died down and everyone went about their business as usual.

Some time after, the news of a new gold strike began to circulate in the area. A man named Samuel Rowland had struck a rich claim on Scottie Creek, about 11 miles from Clinton. As prospectors flocked to the diggings, all thoughts of the gold robbery were quickly forgotten.

To some, however, the rumours of gold on Scottie Creek created interest in an unusual way. Those individuals insisted that there was no gold to be found on Scottie Creek. It had been mined unsuccessfully in the past and abandoned, even by the Chinese, who were always the last to leave a gold-bearing region. When the curious approached Rowland with these ideas however, they found him more cantankerous than most prospectors. He would never allow other prospectors on his claim and kept pretty much to himself. Any miner who had intentions of visiting him for a friendly chat was wary of the Winchester he kept close at hand.

Eventually, news of the strike reached the ears of Chief Const.

Fred Hussey at Kamloops. Hussey also found it odd that Scottie Creek was producing gold. Then, when word reached him that Rowland's claim was the only one yielding gold, his curiosity changed to suspicion. Finally he advised Joe Burr to keep Rowland under surveillance and report on his activities.

One by one the dejected miners withdrew from Scottie Creek. All, that is, except Rowland, who continued to deposit gold at F.W. Foster's general store in Ashcroft. A week later Hussey received word that Rowland's claim had finally played out and that he was preparing to leave. The next stage into Ashcroft brought Hussey, who, after discussing the situation with Burr, decided to arrest Rowland. Armed with a warrant, the two policemen confronted Rowland in his room.

In jail, Rowland was quite willing to offer his written account of how he had come by the gold, and for the better part of a hour he wrote about his discovery. When the completed report was handed to Hussey, his suspicions were confirmed: Rowland, in his written statement, had proved he knew nothing about mining.

The next order of business was to examine the gold. Hussey knew that gold from different countries, regions, or even streams and rivers, were as different as fingerprints; no two have quite the same quality, colour or texture. Dust, flakes, smooth pebbles, coarse nuggets — all these are the results of the water action in which they are found. Hussey hoped that an examination of Rowland's gold would provide some clue as to where it had really come from. For Hussey was convinced it had not been mined on Scottie Creek.

Crossing to Foster's store, Hussey asked to see the bag of gold Rowland had deposited for safekeeping. The Chief Constable then scrutinized the particles with the aid of a magnifying glass.

"Just as I thought," he said, straightening. "This gold came from a dozen different creeks. Have a look."

It did not take Burr long to confirm his Chief's opinion. They had a case.

At the trial, Hussey explained that: "The gold we examined came from several Cariboo Creeks, but generally in the Barkerville region. The only way Mr. Rowland could have come by such a varied accumulation of nuggets is from a strongbox, which could contain gold from many different claims. I suggest Mr. Rowland held-up the stage last July, and then salted Scottie Creek with the loot. He then pretended to wash it out, and was preparing to leave when apprehended."

The jury agreed with Hussey, and Rowland was found guilty and sentenced to five years in the penitentiary at New Westminster.

Discovery Claim on Williams Creek. The gold stolen by Rowland during the stagecoach robbery came from several creeks in the Barkerville area. (Inset) Interior of Gold Commissioner's office, Barkerville.

Shortly after his capture, rumours began to circulate that only $3,000 had been recovered and $12,000 was still missing. It was assumed that Rowland had buried the missing gold bars somewhere on his claim at Scottie Creek until he could return for it at some later date. Barnard's Express supposedly posted a $1,000 reward for information leading to the recovery of the gold bars, but it was never claimed.

Two Chinese miners, Wen Lit Ong and Yeun Low, who had been employed by Rowland on Scottie Creek, began searching the claim for the missing $12,000. They were convinced he had buried it on a knoll overlooking the creek, but their concentrated efforts proved fruitless. Finally winter set in and they were forced to abandon their search until the following spring, when they returned and continued their relentless search. But no trace of the stolen gold bars was ever found.

After serving two years of his sentence, Rowland broke jail and escaped. He was never seen again. Whether or not he returned for the gold bars is debatable, but most sources agree he headed south after his escape and never returned.

ANOTHER VERSION

Another version to this story appeared in a 1948 issue of the *British Columbia Historical Quarterly*. The author, Willis J. West, since deceased, was a one-time employee of Barnard's Express. His version, an excerpt from the longer article entitled "Staging and Stage Hold-up," is written from first-hand knowledge and records. The part concerning the robbery in question is reprinted with the permission of the B.C. Archives, Victoria.

"It is remarkable, considering the value of the gold carried each season, how seldom the Cariboo stage was held-up and robbed during the half century it operated, and for this there are two main reasons; first, the manner in which law and order were administered in Cariboo, and, second, the difficulty of escaping capture and making a safe get-away after the hold-up. In those days there was no delay and no red tape to speak of in punishing a criminal. When a man committed murder he was given a fair trial and hanged with dispatch.

"However, in the original Minute-book of the Company which I have before me as I write there appears the following entry in the minutes of a shareholder's meeting held at Ashcroft on September 16, 1890: 'Regarding the robbery of the stage on the 14th July last near the 99 Mile Post, the shareholders present regret to report any substantial clue to the identity of the perpetrator.' At the next annual meeting of the shareholders held September 14, 1891, the following entry appears in the minutes: 'Satisfaction was expressed at the result of the trial of M.V.B. Rowland, for the robbery of the stage near Bridge Creek in July, 1890, who was convicted to a term in the Provincial penitentiary at New Westminster.'

"Martin Van Buren Rowland had been working in the mines around Barkerville and was on a trip 'outside' travelling by saddlehorse and leading a pack-horse when he conceived the idea of robbing the stage. After his conviction he wrote a confession describing how he left his camp and circled back in the timber, coming out to the road at the foot of Bridge Creek hill while it was still dark. Stages are without exception 'held-up' on hills or on steep pitches so that the stage-driver cannot suddenly whip up his horses in the hope of getting away. Rowland waited for the stage near the 99 mile post where it usually stopped on this 4-mile-long hill to breathe the horses. In his confession he went on to describe how he covered the driver, William Parker, with his rifle and demanded he turn over the stage safe and treasure bag. As Parker was unarmed he was obliged to throw out the treasure bag and get the gold-safe from its compartment under the back seat. Parker was able to talk Rowland into letting him retain the treasure bag by telling him that it contained only waybills and other documents which might get the bandit into trouble if they were found in his possession. Parker had difficulty in getting the bag back on the stage without the bandit noticing its weight. It contained $2,500 worth of gold dust. Rowland also related that after he had ordered the stage to drive on, he loaded the gold-safe on his pack horse and rode some distance up Bridge Creek before dismounting to chop open the back of the safe with his axe and thus extract the gold which was valued at $4,500. Hiding the safe in the heavy brush under a fallen tree, he departed with the gold it had contained. The B.X. obtained a confession from Rowland in an effort to locate the safe and recover the valuable papers which had been locked in it, but their search was in vain.

"Rowland was successful in returning undetected up the road to his camp. He then proceeded at a leisurely rate back down the road past the scene of the robbery and on to Ashcroft. If he had been wise, he would have taken the train out of the country and enjoyed his spoils without ever being suspected of the stagecoach job. As it was he was too clever for his own good, for, after going on a good spree, he bought a stock of grub and let it be known that he was journeying back up the road about 20 miles to Scottie Creek to do some prospecting. There had been several stampedes or excitements over Scottie Creek when a little coarse gold had been found there at different times. Some prospectors, however, had thoroughly tried out the ground and located nothing worthwhile, so it was abandoned. Some time later Rowland went back to Ashcroft and went on another spree, stating that he had found rich ground. He bought more supplies and returned to his camp. The B.X. became a little suspicious and when they later found he had spent some gold dust in the saloons they asked the bar-tenders to save any gold Rowland might tender in payment

Barkerville as it appears today. The gold "mined" by Rowland was proved to come from nearby creeks.

for whisky in the event he came to town again.

"It may not be generally known that gold mined in the creeks varies greatly in color, feel, size, value and so forth, and that any experienced miner or banker could upon examining any gold-dust, tell from which creek it had come from. As Rowland did not again visit Ashcroft, a sample of the gold he was spending could not be checked to see if it was stolen gold. He remained at Scottie Creek some weeks and then one day startled the driver of the regular mail stage by tendering a shipment of gold, a little over $4,000 in value, which he claimed he had mined at Scottie Creek and wished to have delivered to the Gold Commissioner at Barkerville with the request it be melted down to bullion. Upon delivery it was identified by the Gold Commissioner as the stolen gold in the Bridge Creek hill robbery and Rowland was immediately arrested, convicted, and sentenced. He was not convicted of the robbery — since it took place in the dark and he could not be positively identified — but for having in his possession stolen gold for which he could not account."

SUMMARY AND CONCLUSION

Mr. West's account of the robbery and the events that followed conflict with the original legend, and casts serious doubts as to the existence of a buried treasure.

(1) Although the Tingley family owned the B.X. at the time of the robbery, the stage driver on the day in question was William Parker, not Steve Tingley.

(2) The strongbox was not found by the posse, but was only recovered years later by railway workers.

(3) There were no passengers in the stage on the day of the robbery.

(4) It was the Gold Commissioner who identified the gold, not Hussey.

(5) West referred to the robber as Martin Van Buren Rowland, not Samuel Rowland as is commonly written.

(6) Rowland sent his stolen gold to Barkerville for safekeeping, not Ashcroft as reported in many accounts.

(7) The amount of gold taken in the robbery totalled only $4,500, not $15,000 as was reported.

(8) The amount of gold finally recovered was just over $4,000.

(9) No gold bars are mentioned in the robbery.

While some of these contradictions can be explained by the constant retelling of the story, others cannot. Regardless of this, items 1 to 6 are minor points and do not prove or disprove anything substantial. Items 7, 8 and 9 however, are damning. Remembering that the second version was written by a one-time employee of Barnard's Express, from Company records and first-hand knowledge, it must be assumed basically correct. It must be concluded, therefore, that the robbery netted Rowland only $4,500. Of this amount, $4,000 was eventually recovered. The remaining $500 can easily be explained by Rowland's two spending sprees and his purchase of grub and supplies.

It is highly unlikely, therefore, that this treasure exists, and treasure hunters should concentrate their efforts on lost treasures that do.

12

LOST KLONDIKE GOLD

The summit of the Chilkoot Pass, well known for its fierce blizzards, is the repository of two lost gold shipments. Each were abandoned by prospectors trying to save something more valuable — their lives.

THROUGH the Golden Gate and into the beautiful waters of San Francisco Bay steamed the little ship *Excelsior* on the morning of July 14, 1897. Aboard were 40 hardy souls who months or years before had gone into the frozen north to wrest their fortune from the hands of fate. This vanguard of fortune seekers brought with them $500,000 worth of gold. Not one carried less than $5,000, and some had as much as $90,000. This wealth varied in size from nuggets as large as hazelnuts down through various sizes to the proverbial dust. It was carried loose in pockets, in tin cans, in canvas bags, in wooden boxes and some of it was even wrapped up in brown paper.

Two days later the *Portland* docked carrying another 68 miners and over $700,000 in gold. When the news of these two ships spread, it electrified the world, changed the course of history, and put the previously unknown hinterland of what was to become Yukon Territory on the map.

For all intents and purposes, the arrival of these two treasure-laden ships signalled the start of the Klondike gold rush, the largest the world had ever seen. But it was not the first time gold had been discovered in the Yukon, or, for that matter, the first gold rush to take place there.

Robert Campbell, one of the Hudson's Bay Company's (HBC) most industrious employees, had discovered traces of gold around Fort Selkirk as early as 1847. But the HBC was interested in furs, not gold, so the discovery was ignored. In 1863, Rev. Robert McDonald found gold on Birch Creek, just upriver from Fort Yukon. When he sent samples of coarse gold back to England, the London *Times* published an account of his discovery, but no one else paid much attention.

It was the discovery of lode gold near Juneau in 1880 that would indirectly lead to the rich Yukon goldfields. The discovery at Juneau attracted drifters, frontiersmen and adventures from all over the American west. Gradually, in twos and threes, they drifted northward into the Yukon Valley. By 1886, some 200 miners had crossed the Chilkoot Pass and had worked their way 300 miles down the Yukon River to the mouth of the Stewart River, where, in a single year, they had recovered $100,000 worth of gold dust. To service these prospectors, LeRoy "Jack" McQuesten and Arthur Harper built a trading post at the mouth of the Stewart River. Then, anticipating an active trade for 1887, McQuesten left for San Francisco to order more supplies.

Meanwhile, on September 7, 1885, Howard Franklin had decided to try his luck on Forty Mile Creek, about 100 miles downstream from Stewart. Camping on the banks of the Yukon River, he walked about two miles upstream until he found exposed bedrock. Then he removed a shovelful of dirt from a crevice which, when panned, yielded a half ounce of coarse nuggets. When Franklin returned to Stewart with the gleaming nuggets in the winter of 1886, the camp was electrified. These were the elusive nuggets they had been searching for. Abandoning Stewart River almost to a man, the miners prepared to follow Franklin back to Forty Mile.

This was exciting news for all concerned, but it created a dilemma for Harper. He knew that when news of this rich new discovery reached the outside, hundreds of miners would rush in. While this was good for business, it also caused a serious problem: there was not enough supplies to feed the expected stampede. Harper would somehow have to get word to McQuesten to substantially increase his order or there would be starvation in the Yukon. But how could he notify McQuesten? It was winter; the Yukon River was frozen solid, and all communication with the outside world was cut off. The nearest point of civilization was John Healey's trading post on the far side of the Chilkoot Mountains on Dyea Inlet. In between lay 500 miles of hostile wilderness few men had navigated in winter. Who would be brave or foolish enough to take out Harper's message?

Thomas Williams, a river-boat pilot employed with the Alaska Commercial Company, volunteered. Williams had entered the Yukon by way of St. Michaels and had never travelled over the route he was now agreeing to tackle. Yet, despite warnings from friends that the journey was far too dangerous, and that there were no roadhouses where he could rest or replenish his supplies, Williams was determined to try.

Aided only by some crude maps and accompanied by an Indian boy who had never been over the route either, Williams loaded a mail sack on a dog sled and left Stewart on December 3. In the sack, in addition to letters from the Alaska Commercial Company

The lure of gold tempted many to challenge the notorious Chilkoot Pass. (Inset) The remains of the old tramway cable near the top of Chilkoot Pass in

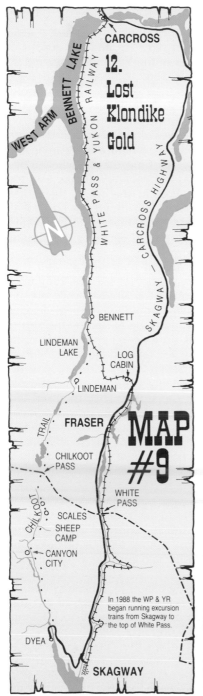

Map labels:
WEST ARM · BENNETT LAKE · CARCROSS · **12. Lost Klondike Gold** · WHITE PASS & YUKON RAILWAY · CARCROSS HIGHWAY · SKAGWAY – CARCROSS · BENNETT · LINDEMAN LAKE · LOG CABIN · LINDEMAN · TRAIL · FRASER · CHILKOOT PASS · **MAP #9** · WHITE PASS · CHILKOOT · SCALES · SHEEP CAMP · CANYON CITY · In 1988 the WP & YR began running excursion trains from Skagway to the top of White Pass. · DYEA · SKAGWAY

(Above) Arthur Harper. When coarse gold was discovered on Forty Mile River, he sent Thomas Williams to the "outside" with a message for McQuesten to purchase more supplies.

(Below) John J. Healey. It was to his trading post at Dyea that Williams and the Indian were heading with Harper's message, some mail, and about 176 ounces in gold.

to its head office in San Francisco, was about $3,000 in gold.

The journey, as expected, was a most difficult one. In the dead of winter ". . .over the hummocks of river ice and the copses of fallen trees, through the cold jungles of the Yukon forests, and up the slippery flanks of the mountains" they trudged onward. Even before they reached the mountains their dogs had died of cold, exhaustion or hunger, and Williams and the Indian boy, now out of provisions, were forced to eat them to survive.

Now on foot, lugging the mail sack, weakened by cold and hunger, they clawed their way up the Chilkoot summit and straight into the teeth of a vicious blizzard. By the time they reached Stone House, so named from a large mass or rocks, Williams was too exhausted to continue. Digging a hole in the snow, the Indian fashioned some kind of shelter into which they crawled to wait out the storm. Without food or heat, they shivered in their snow house for three days, during which time their faces, hands and feet became blackened by frostbite.

On the fourth day the weather abated only slightly, but they knew that if they were to have any chance of survival they must reach Dyea soon. With Williams already too weak to walk, the boy hoisted him to his shoulders and began the long descent, leaving the mail sack and its gold dust behind to be buried by the storm. When the exhausted Indian could no longer carry Williams, he dropped him in the snow and struggled onward alone. The future of both men looked bleak until, at Sheep Camp, a rest stop at the edge of the tree line, the boy suddenly came upon a group of prospectors who were waiting out the storm. They followed him back up the mountain and helped bring Williams down to Sheep Camp where he was revived with hot soup. The courageous Indian then borrowed a sled and dragged the barely conscious Williams the remaining 26 miles to Healey's trading post at Dyea. But it was too late for Williams. He died two days later without regaining consciousness.

Healey and the men in the post were naturally anxious to learn what life-or-death mission had inspired this race over the Chilkoot Pass in the dead of winter. The Indian, knowing few words of English, glanced around the room. Seeing a sack of beans on Healey's counter, he grabbed a handful and flung them on the floor, saying: "Gold. All same as this!"

The Indian boy was then taken by canoe to Juneau where his frozen toes were amputated. With him travelled news of the gold strike along with a few loose letters that had been on Williams' body. When news of the discovery on Forty Mile Creek reached Victoria, about 500 people started off for the Yukon goldfields in its first gold rush.

SUMMARY AND CONCLUSION

To my knowledge, this is the first time that the tragedy of the

Williams expedition has been referred to as a treasure story. Yet, although there are some minor variations, all of the events related up to this point actually happened. I came upon the possibility of this lost treasure quite by accident while doing some research on the Yukon gold rush. The specific reference which attracted my attention was found in a book written by J. Bernard Moore.

J.B. Moore was the son of the famous William Moore, river-boat captain, gold seeker, and the founder of Skagway. Bernard was 21 years of age when news of the gold discovery on Forty Mile Creek reached him in Victoria in the spring of 1887. On March 11, he joined about 500 other miners who, upon hearing the exciting news, were in the vanguard of this first Yukon gold rush. Bernard died in San Francisco in 1919, but in 1968 his diary, chronicling his adventures in the Yukon, was published in *Skagway in Days Primeval.* Moore's account is the only one which specifically mentions the presence of gold in the mail sack, and then only in passing, when he wrote: ". . .the mail pouch which, we learned afterwards, contained $3,000 in gold dust was also lost and buried in the snow."

Pierre Burton, writing about the Klondike gold rush in *Klondike,* mentions the events surrounding the death of Williams without commenting in any way on the contents of the mail pouch. In fact, Burton does not even mention the existence of the mail pouch itself, which we know existed, in his version. Likewise, T.W. Paterson, writing about Yukon ghost towns in his book *Ghost Towns of the Yukon,* does not get specific about the contents of the mail pouch either. So, the first question we must concern ourselves with is, was there or was there not gold included in the mail pouch?

In *Ghost Towns of the Yukon* Paterson quotes Howard Franklin, whose discovery at Forty Mile provided the impetus for the dangerous trek in the first place, as stating that the coarse gold which he recovered from Franklin Bar ". . .was given to Harper and Mayo, who dispatched Williams and an Indian to Dyea, the former to San Francisco, to tell Jack McQuestin (sic) about the find that had been made. They left Stewart on December 3, and were caught in a storm on the summit. Williams died of exposure and the Indian had a narrow escape, only reaching Dyea with great difficulty. Men went to the summit, got Williams' mail, and at a miner's meeting it was decided to open the letters and see what news had been sent out."

We know that Harper dispatched Williams to take out news of the gold discovery, but even Franklin's account does not clarify for certain whether or not any gold was included with the mail. Thus Moore's diary remains the only account which specifically mentions the presence of gold in the mail pouch. Since his diary was not published until long after his death, one must ask oneself, why would Moore make such an entry unless he believed it to be true? Naturally, it would be nice to verify the gold from other sources, but, unless evidence to refute the claim is found, it is certainly reasonable to assume that gold was included in the mail pouch.

If we accept the possible existence of the gold, how do we calculate its present value? Moore placed the value of the gold at $3,000. Since gold was worth about $17 an ounce at the time, the pouch must have contained 176 ounces. Based on today's value of about $500 an ounce, the original gold shipment would now be worth $88,000.

Next we must try to establish whether or not the gold was actually lost, and if so, where. Moore claims that the mail pouch was left behind at the Stone House, lost and buried by a snowdrift. Although Burton does not refer to the mail pouch at all, he agrees that the men at Healey's trading post learned of the rich strike by the Indian's dramatic illustration with a handful of beans. This would not appear necessary if the mail pouch had not been lost, so Burton's version would tend to substantiate that the mail sack was not with Williams and the Indian when they reached Dyea.

Paterson also claims that the mail sack was left behind on the mountain, but he goes on to state that "the miners then went up the mountainside and recovered the mail sack." This assumption is undoubtedly based on Franklin's previously stated remarks that "Men went to the summit, got Williams' mail, and at a miners' meeting it was decided to open the letters and see what news had been sent out." If Franklin is correct, then our lost gold was probably recovered with the mail.

However, don't be too disheartened, for the Chilkoot is apparently the repository of not one but at least two lost gold shipments, the second one far more substantial. According to Burton's *Klondike,* "The only winter route to the outside world was the grueling trek upstream to the Chilkoot, more than six hundred miles distant (from Forty Mile). After Williams death it was seldom attempted. Four men who tried it in 1893 were forced to abandon fifteen thousand dollars in gold dust on the mountain slopes and were so badly crippled by the elements that one died and another was incapacitated for life."

Did the two remaining men return for their gold, currently valued at over $400,000? Did they find it? Who knows?

The Chilkoot Pass was a tortuous ordeal suffered by thousands of gold-crazed individuals who sought the richness of the Klondike. Many never made it over the summit. Discouraged by the terrible hardship, they returned home disheartened and dejected. Others died on the trail. Many threw aside items of value that were simply too heavy to carry over the icy slopes. Is it too preposterous to assume that, of all the thousands who passed this way, not a few cached valuables of some sort along the trail, hoping one day to

When the tidal community of Dyea, Alaska became the jumping-off point for the Chilkoot Trail, thousands of adventurers transformed the mouth of the Dyea River into a city of canvas and supplies, as shown here. Everything shown in the photograph was packed over the mountains on a man's back, or by pack animal.

return and reclaim them? The Chilkoot Trail is still littered with a variety of items and artifacts from this gold-crazed era. These relics, crumbling and decaying, remain in plain view exactly where they were discarded so many years before. If they could talk what wonderful tales they could tell; of hardship, perseverance, hopes and shattered dreams. Who knows, someday someone might stumble across the hard-won fortune of some unfortunate prospector, who, having wrested the treasure from the frozen Klondike, had to abandon it along the summit in a desperate attempt to save something even more valuable, his life.

13

McLEOD'S MISSING MILLIONS

According to legend, discoverers Willie and Frank McLeod were the first of some 20 people who have been murdered or disappeared while searching for a rich gold mine in Nahanni National Park.

McLEOD'S Lode; McClouds Missing Millions; Lost Gold of Shangri-La Valley; these are but a few of the colourful names (and spellings) which have been attached to one of northern Canada's legendary lost treasures.

Like all good treasure tales, the facts concerning this lost lode in the Northwest Territories have been all but lost in the haze of legends which have been circulating and growing, during the past three-quarters of a century. In fact, no two writers seem to agree on much beyond the fact that, "somewhere in the northern reaches of Canada," a fabulously rich gold mine, its history tainted with murder, awaits some lucky discoverer.

What most do not tell you, is that the Northwest Territories, as a glance at a map will show, covers a lot of ground; something like 1.5 million square miles — almost half of Canada! This vast size, coupled with a total population of less than 50,000 persons (smaller than the average Canadian city), and some of the roughest terrain on the North American continent, makes searching for a lost gold mine seem not only impossible, but insane. It also is dangerous, as, according to popular legend, the search for this particular mine has claimed no fewer than 20 lives to date.

ORIGINAL LEGEND

One popular version has it that the stories of gold along the reaches of the Nahanni River began as early as 1900, when a Nahanni Indian first appeared at a Hudson's Bay Company (HBC) trading post with a sackful of gold chunks, which he spent with the abandon of a man who knew where to get plenty more. Although the rich brave was careful not to say too much to the white trappers and prospectors who crowded around him, he let it be known that he had found his gold in the dense wilderness south of the junction of the Flat and South Nahanni rivers, a dense, unknown region just south of the Yukon boundary which had not known the presence of a white man since a handful of adventurers passed through on their way to the Klondike, several years before. Those who knew of this country spoke of treacherous rivers, with giant eddies that could swallow an entire canoe and its occupants; of muskeg that was every bit as treacherous as quicksand; of mosquitoes and blackflies that could eat a man alive. As if to write off the no-man's-land completely, native superstition included a curse, local Indians whispering of a valley haunted by evil spirits, from which mere mortals did not return.

This valley, the "Shangri-La" of modern-day legend, supposedly was an oasis in the northland, with hot mineral springs and subtropical temperatures. When the surrounding mountains and valleys were deep in the subarctic snows, the evil valley reputedly remained warm and green, its demons constantly on the prowl.

As for the Indian brave with the poke of nuggets, he seemed to have defied the tribal legends and, like true prospectors of all races, squandered his wealth on wine, women and song until broke. However, unlike the usual protagonists of good treasure stories, who go to the well once too often, he seems to have enjoyed his fling, then, sated, returned to his usual occupation as hunter and trapper. Within three years, his short-lived "gold rush" was forgotten by all but a few die-hard prospectors.

Not until 1903, when another Indian appeared with a poke of raw gold did the stories of a lost, and fabulously rich, gold mine begin to circulate the north country. This time, at least, storytellers had a little more to go on, as this native had cheerfully revealed the source of his find as Bennett Creek, a tributary of Flat River. Like the nearby South Nahanni, this, too, was forbidden country to Indians. Yet, for a second time, a brave had defied tribal taboo and had been rewarded with nuggets of gold. This time the Nahanni's fame as a source of wealth was assured, as word spread of the wonderful valley where the sun always shone, and where steaming water from hot springs trickled over creek-beds yellow with gold.

But, for all of the colourful stories being passed around, it remained for two brothers named McLeod to begin the search which goes on to this day. The half-breed sons of a Fort Liard factor for the HBC, Willie and Frank listened to the stories with growing interest, becoming convinced that, with any luck at all, men with their bush experience and stamina could find the lost lode, thought to be at the southern end of the forbidding MacKenzie Mountain Range.

For some reason, the brothers began their first expedition at Telegraph Creek, in British Columbia, travelling overland to Flat River, the Nahanni's biggest tributary, by way of Dease Lake. It

(Above) The confluence of the Flat and Nahanni rivers.
(Opposite page) Pulpit Rock and the Gate of the South Nahanni River.

was as they worked their way along the Flat that they encountered a party of Cassiar Indians, who, they later reported, had been prospecting with some success. Frank later claimed that the natives had shown him nuggets the size of chicken eggs!

More than ever convinced that they were on the trail of Mother Fortune, the brothers tried to learn from the Indians where they had found their gold. But the Cassiars were vague, and the brothers learned little. After searching the immediate vicinity without success, they pushed on to the junction of Bennett Creek and Flat River. It was in this area, so the story goes, that Frank and Willie McLeod struck paydirt. In the short time remaining before the onslaught of winter, they collected a large array of samples until, running dangerously short of supplies, they had no choice but to head downstream.

Constructing a crude scow from abandoned sluice boxes in the area, they poled their way downstream until a treacherous rapid known as the Cascade of the Thirteen Drops capsized their boat. Although they escaped with only a dunking, and succeeded in righting their boat, they had lost their precious cargo. Thus, when the brothers reached Fort Liard, hungry and tired, they were again broke.

Even with the knowledge of a rich gold mine, they had to eat, and, that winter, they earned a grubstake for their next expedition by working for the HBC. Impatient to head back to Flat River, they worked hard and saved their wages. But despite their attempts to keep their gold mine a secret, word of their successful trip spread. The brothers began to enjoy their new-found notoriety, and entertained one and all with incredible stories of a tropical valley and the South Nahanni River, which they described as being one of the most beautiful stretches of waterways they had ever seen. The strange valley, they said, was always warm, heated by numerous hot springs and inhabited by all manner of wildlife, including exotic birds and butterflies.

Most listeners must have received the McLeod's weird tales with reservation, few believing that such a valley could exist in the cold northern reaches of the MacKenzie. Only one man, identified as a Scottish engineer named Wilkinson (or Weir), expressed full confidence in the brother's stories. Not only did he believe every word they said, but he wanted to accompany them on their next expedition. Curiously, Willie and Frank accepted this offer, perhaps deciding that an extra strong back would be of valuable use in the bush. Undoubtedly, Wilkinson's arrival meant a welcome boost to their grubstake as well, enabling them to head into the wilds that much sooner.

Whatever, Wilkinson joined the team and, in the spring of 1905, the three partners set out to find their fortunes.

The summer passed, and it was autumn. Then winter. Yet the McLeods and Wilkinson failed to appear at Fort Liard as scheduled. When the spring and summer of 1906 slipped by, with winter once again approaching, a third brother, Charlie, began to grow concerned. However, it was a big country, and one rich in game. Willie and Frank were expert woodsmen, and well experienced at living off the land. If anyone could survive the brutal northern winters, he was sure his brothers could.

But another year passed, and Willie, Frank and Wilkinson failed to show. Not until the spring of 1908, three full years after they set out on their second expedition to Flat River, did Charlie McLeod decide to go in search. A veteran outdoorsman himself, he had no difficulty in following their proposed route to the Flat River. On the rare occasions that he encountered a trapper or Indian hunter, he asked if they had seen three white prospectors. But the answer was always a silent shaking of the head.

For months, Charlie pressed onward, until he observed the entrance to a large valley. Although running short of time, he remembered his brothers' glowing tales of a strange valley and decided to give it a cursory examination before heading back to civilization. As he paddled along, he became vaguely aware that the valley was different to the others he had explored. Here, it seemed warmer, the vegetation along the river-banks seeming to grow thicker.

When Charlie noticed a small clearing in the trees, he turned the bow of his canoe shoreward, his curiosity piqued that, at this one particular spot in the lush growth, no trees grew. He had no sooner stepped onto the river-bank when he spotted the remains of an old sled runner in the grass. Upon picking it up, he was amazed to see that it bore writing: a carefully pencilled scrawl which he immediately knew to be that of one of his brothers. Undated, brief and to the point, the message read: "We have found a fine prospect."

Although he searched the old campsite diligently, there was not another clue to be found. But at least he knew that Willie and Frank had been there, that he was on the right track.

Eagerly, Charlie pushed deeper into the valley. Some distance downstream, he sighted the obvious remains of another campsite and landed. The first thing to catch his eyes was a rusted rifle leaning against a tree. A few feet away were two old bedrolls that unmistakably had belonged to his brothers.

But it was his third discovery that staggered him. For, beneath the bedrolls lay two skeletons. Charlie had found his brothers.

Upon overcoming his horror, Charlie forced himself to examine the campsite and vicinity. However, no other clues were to be found. Of Wilkinson, the Scottish engineer, there was not a trace, and he sadly returned to Fort Liard to report his brothers' deaths to the authorities.

When Mounties returned to the death camp with Charlie, they, too, were unprepared for the scene which awaited them. For, in his haste, and the horror, of discovering his brothers' remains, Charlie had overlooked one terrifying item: the fact that both skulls were missing.

Today, the legends of the McLeod's deaths, and of their having been decapitated, have not only inspired a number of fascinating, if doubtful stories, but have changed the map. To this day, Deadman's Valley denotes the area in which their bodies were found, three-quarters of a century ago.

The policemen's immediate reaction was that the remains had been mutilated by animals. But the fact that the skeletons were intact, and still in their bedrolls, seemed to outrule this possibility. Throughout his life, Charlie McLeod maintained that the decapitations had been almost surgically neat. It was his firm belief that his brothers had been murdered in their sleep by the missing Wilkinson, who had removed the heads so as to conceal the bullet wounds. As an arm of one of the skeletons appeared to be reaching for the nearby rifle at the moment of death, murder seemed to be the inevitable verdict, and that which most familiar with the story accept to this day.

The deceptively beautiful First Canyon of Nahanni National Park.

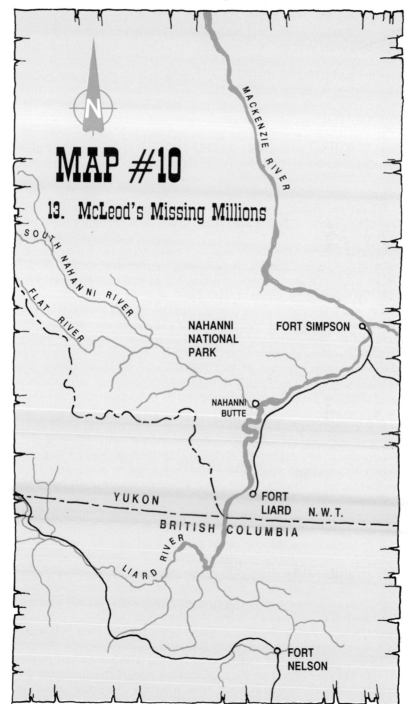

MAP #10

13. McLeod's Missing Millions

A thorough search of the old campsite turned up several pieces of gold-bearing quartz, but nothing rich enough to justify murder. This also indicated to Charlie McLeod that his brothers were killed, the fruits of their labours packed away by the murderer. A final curious fact was that the brothers' picks and shovels were not to be found. To Charlie, this meant beyond a shadow of a doubt that Willie and Frank struck it rich, that their tools remained at the minesite which must be nearby.

The Mounties reserved judgement, unwilling to rule out the possibility that the brothers had died of natural causes. They also thought it possible that the McLeods could have been murdered along with Wilkinson, despite the absence of his *corpus delecti,* by Indians; or for that matter, by almost anyone.

Whatever, Willie and Frank McLeod were buried beside the turbulent Nahanni. But if they were gone, they certainly were not to be forgotten.

Charlie McLeod definitely was not about to forget his brothers, or their gold mine. Staunchly believing that he deserved to find it if anyone did, he proceeded to express his view at every opportunity that the missing Scotchman, Wilkinson, had murdered Willie and Frank, and formulated plans to return to Deadman's Valley. Because of the macabre events surrounding his brothers' deaths, and his own vocal efforts, the legend of Deadman's or "Headless" Valley and its murderous mine soon achieved international status, no self-respecting magazine or newspaper turning down an opportunity to tell and retell the story of the tropical valley where gold could be picked up from the ground, and where men vanished by the score.

Ironically, the articles began to prove themselves prophetic when prospectors, many of them inexperienced and ill-equipped, proceeded to search for the McLeod's, by then, legendary lode. As was to be expected, impatience and inexperience in country such as this could lead only to tragedy. The fact that few prospectors bothered to report their safe return to civilization only added to the number of those thought to have gone missing. Combined with the increased reluctance of Indians to travel through the region, the Nahanni's reputation as a jinxed, and deadly, river grew steadily.

Most of those determined to flaunt the curse of Headless Valley began their expeditions at Fort Nelson, B.C., where they could hire experienced crews and flat-bottomed river boats, or buy canoes, for the 100-mile voyage down the Fort Nelson River to Nelson Forks, where they entered the Liard River for the final 200 miles of smooth passage to the South Nahanni.

There, the going got rough, with furious whirlpools and rapids which did everything in their power to smash the adventurers' craft against the canyon walls that towered vertically from the river's edge. Fortunately, between such obstacle courses, the river was relatively easy to navigate, and offered those who survived the rapids, sights that were as spectacular as any on the continent, including a waterfall more than 1,000 feet high, and the "Shortest river in the world;" an underground stream that broke the surface just 75 feet from its junction with the Nahanni.

Making life all the more difficult for the prospector was the fact the Nahanni then split into six channels, of which all but two were false leads. Many of those making the trip for the first time lost precious days in navigating the maze before being able to continue down river, where most overlooked the entrance to Deadman's Valley. Those who did succeed in probing the valley's mouth, faced their next obstacle in not knowing precisely where the McLeods had made their last, fatal camp. If, as Charlie McLeod believed to his dying day, Willie and Frank had struck it rich, it is reasonable to conclude that their mine lies within a short distance of their campsite. Those who travelled so far, and against such obstacles, only to miss the site entirely, could hardly have hoped to find the mine, which remained a tantalizing mystery.

One man is thought to have found the McLeod treasure; at least, it is known that he found gold. Unfortunately, he also found sudden death.

Martin Jorgenson, a Swede, arrived on the scene the following year. Inspired by the ever-growing tales of a rich mine somewhere along the banks, or tributaries, of the South Nahanni, and grubstaked by an ex-Mountie named Poole Field, he set out into the wilderness. For two years, Field, then a trader at Ross River, heard not a word from the prospector. Then, much to his surprise and delight, a passing Indian delivered a hastily-scribbled note. The message was from Jorgenson, who breathlessly told of having struck it rich. For Field's benefit, Jorgenson included a crude map showing the location of his cabin on the South Nahanni, and urged him to come at once.

When the Indian courier displayed the nuggets that Jorgenson had given him as payment for delivering the letter, Field immediately resolved to accept the Swede's invitation and see the claim for himself. But, when Field stepped ashore at the site which Jorgenson had indicated as his camp, he was astonished to find the prospector's cabin burned to the ground. He was even more astonished when, nearby, he found a human skeleton, a broken rifle and two spent cartridges. The remains, he was sure, were those of Martin Jorgenson. But how he died, the story behind the broken rifle and spent shells, has never been answered; nor, for that matter, has the mystery of Jorgenson's reputed claim. For, in his letter to Field, he gave no details as to its location, and his map had merely shown his benefactor how to find the cabin. If Jorgenson had, in fact found the lost McLeod lode, he, too, took

(Above) Virginia Falls Rapids, Nahanni National Park.
(Below) Upper Nahanni River, Deadman Valley, in September, 1976.

the secret to his grave.

The list of casualties, in and about the South Nahanni, grew steadily. In many instances, any link between the disappearance or death, and the lost gold mine seems tenuous at best. But in 1931, a trapper named Phil Powers had let it be known that he was going in search of the treasure. Police, informed that he had not reappeared, instituted a search and found his remains. As in the case of Martin Jorgenson, his cabin had been burned to the ground. When discovered, a revolver lay within a few feet of the skeleton. Each of its six chambers had been fired; at least according to legend, if not record.

And so it went, although, usually, those who fell victim to the "curse" did so under natural circumstances. Newspapers and magazines continued to reap sensational copy, and the legends of Deadman's, or "Headless" Valley, and of a malevolent force that haunted white intruders, grew and grew.

One of those who did invade the valley, on several occasions, and live, was Charlie McLeod. Unable to turn his back on the valley that had claimed the lives of his brothers, and unwilling to resist the lure of their supposed mine, he made two further expeditions, spaced many years apart, to the Nahanni. Years before, the RCMP tentatively identified newly-found human remains as those of Wilkinson, the missing Scotsman, and had concluded that he, and Willie and Frank McLeod died by starvation, the brothers' remains having been mutilated by bears. Despite their verdict, Charlie refused to believe that Wilkinson, or Weir, was dead, and cited reports from his own investigations that indicated the missing prospector had been seen several times in Vancouver, and elsewhere, and that he had carried a fortune in gold out of the north country.

Through hundreds of inquiries and untiring research over the years, Charlie became convinced that his brothers' mine would be found on Sheep Creek, near Flat River, which pours into the Nahanni but a few miles from the McLeods' last camp. But, with a growing family, he confined himself to asking questions and repeating his charge that Wilkinson had murdered his brothers, until 1942, when, with several others he explored the banks of Sheep Creek. Although the party did find gold, and some copper, it was not the rich lode that Charlie was convinced his brothers had found, and he returned to his home in Alberta, as frustrated as ever.

In 1950, with his three sons, the determined Charlie McLeod made a last, determined attack on Sheep Creek, now known as McCloud Creek, in misspelled honour of his brothers. To the son's surprise, they found the Nahanni of evil repute, the so-called "Dark River of Fear," to be a beautiful and rugged river. At the camp where the mutilated skeletons of uncles Willie and Frank had been found, they discovered that the shifting of the river had long since washed away the graves. Despite an exhaustive search of both Flat River and Sheep Creek, the second generation McLeod party found little evidence of a fabulously rich mine, although there were ample signs of placer gold and copper about. This was the last time that Charlie McLeod ventured into the wilds of the Nahanni and Deadman's Valley. Despite his own lack of success, however, Charlie maintained until his dying day that, when found, the McLeod Mine would be somewhere near McCloud Creek.

SUMMARY AND CONCLUSION

An authority on the South Nahanni and surrounding wilderness was the late R.M. Patterson, who first ventured into this region, against the advice of all who knew of his plan, over 50 years ago. His subsequent book, *The Dangerous River,* now a classic of the Canadian North, established him as an author, and has been reprinted many times over the years.

According to Patterson, it had been rumoured that the McLeod brothers learned of gold somewhere along the Flat River from an Indian their father had befriended years before. Outfitting in Vancouver, the three McLeods, Willie, Frank and Charlie, proceeded to Wrangell, Alaska, by steamer. Heading up the frozen Stikine River by dogteam, they fought their way through midwinter to Telegraph Creek, then on to the north end of Dease Lake before following Dease River through the Cassiar Mountains to Liard Plain. Finally, after having overcome every obstacle winter in the north could throw at them, the determined trio reached the upper Flat River.

There, at last, their ordeal was rewarded with an encounter with Cassiar Indians, who showed them large, coarse nuggets worth up to $3 each (something less than the legendary nuggets as big as hen's eggs, but respectable, nevertheless). As it was now spring, the brothers decided to try their own hand at panning the stream, which they exuberantly christened Gold Creek. The Cassiars, apparently content with having had first crack at the creekbed, and likely less than enchanted with the McLeod's arrival, moved on to fresher fields. But, despite much hard work, and the use of the Indians' abandoned sluice-boxes, the brothers found only enough gold to fill a tiny bottle.

As the season was advancing, they agreed to head for home and constructed a crude boat from the sluice-boxes. However, upon being capsized in the infamous Cascades of the Thirteen Drops (Flat River Canyon), they lost everything but a rifle and several shells and returned to their original camp on Gold Creek. Spirits revived after shooting a moose, they did some more panning and sluicing before building a second scow from other sluice-boxes, and tried again to descend the treacherous Flat. This time, they made it home to Fort Liard without mishap.

The next year, convinced that they would have better luck, Willie,

Frank and an "unnamed" Scottish engineer decided to return to Flat River. When they failed to come out, Charlie, in due course, found their remains. Although popular legend has it that they had been decapitated, Patterson said that he had also been told many times that, when found, the McLeods' skeletons had been tied to trees. As Patterson noted, it was highly unlikely that the remains would have lain undisturbed for three years. As he knew all to well, the country was alive with bears and wolves, which would undoubtedly have mutilated the bodies and ransacked the campsite.

Curiously, it had remained for adventurer-author Patterson, in 1952, to formally ask the RCMP just what conclusion they had come to, in the case of the ill-fated McLeods, 46 years before. The Ottawa department of records promptly replied that, according to its investigations of 1909, and a review of the case made in 1921, the McLeods died of starvation and exposure after having set out from Fort Liard with insufficient food and equipment.

As for Jorgenson, the other prospector supposedly murdered, the RCMP stated flatly that it had no record whatever of his having been declared missing, let alone murdered. Thus, almost half a century after, Patterson seems to have publicly stamped "case closed" on both files, thanks to the RCMP's records department.

He also, as much as any other man, laid to rest the legend that no white man survived the South Nahanni's curse. Patterson survived the so-called jinx not once, but three times. He did admit, however, that several others were not as fortunate, although he listed their deaths as being accidental, or the result of inexperience, or overconfidence. After he retired in Victoria, Patterson told this writer that he disagreed with the RCMP verdict of death by starvation as far as the McLeods were concerned. He had, he said, camped on the spot where the brothers died, in 1928, although he had been unaware of the campsite's grim history at the time. He gave it as his opinion that Willie and Frank McLeod were indeed murdered, but by whom, and for what purpose, he did not say.

As for the McLeods' fabulous gold mine, he saw not a sign. Others, over the years, have claimed to have made good showings along the tributaries of the South Nahanni and Flat rivers. But none seems to have struck it rich and, after the inevitable headlines, silence again returns to the mysterious north country where the McLeods met their fate, from whatever cause, three-quarters of a century ago.

But as long as the legends of the McLeods, and Deadmen's (or Headless) Valley, live, the search for their reputed treasure will go on. And, just as likely, the casualty list will grow.

APPENDIX

BRADY & GAY
ATTORNEYS AT LAW,
ROOMS 11 TO 14 ROXWELL BUILDING,
COR. FIRST AVE. AND COLUMBIA ST. TELEPHONE MAIN 143.

SEATTLE, WASHINGTON, *December 11th, 1896.*

Hon. Arthur G. Smith,
  Deputy Attorney General,
    Victoria, B.C.

Dear sir:-

Our client, Mrs. Mary Roderick, widow of the late Mathew Roderick, who met his death at Camp McKinney in Boundary Creek District, Province of British Columbia, on the night of October 26th, 1896, has instructed us to write to you requesting an investigation at your hands.

Mrs. Mary Roderick has this day in our Courts been duly appointed administratrix of the estate of the said Mathew Roderick, and is now the legally authorised agent of said estate, and being his widow and the mother of his children, has that personal interest in the estate which is recognized by humanity everywhere as being the right to have her request given respectful and careful attention.

Mr. Mathew Roderick, as we have been informed, met his death on the night stated at the hands of one J.P. Keane, who was foreman of the mine. Mrs. Roderick sent an agent, one James Conway, a citizen of Seattle and a gentleman whom we know to be of the highest character, to Camp McKinney to make investigation at Camp McKinney. He met the Coroner who held the investigation, one R.W. Jakes, who informed Mr. Conway that he had great trouble to get a jury, that many of the miners stated to him or his officer selecting the jury, that they had already formed an opinion that the killing of Mathew Roderick was unwarranted, and they were therefore excused. The jury, as we have been informed, who did hold the inquest were composed of employees of the Camp McKinney mine, and they exonerated Keane for this killing, which was in obedience to the express desire of the mine owners.

Mr. Mathew Roderick was an American citizen, and went to Camp McKinney in the prosecution of business, and from all information we have been able to gather, at the time of his death he was peaceably pursuing his way, committing no overt acts, and not in any respect violating or attempting to violate any of the laws of your country. It is alleged that Mr. Roderick had upon his person at the time of his death a revolver pistol and a rifle. Mr. Conway who went there and made an examination, discovered that the pistol was not loaded and had not been loaded; that the rifle was not loaded, neither did it have any loads in its magazine; that upon the person of Mr. Roderick was not found any cartridges that would fit the pistol, but that there was a new box, unopened, of cartridges of the same calibre as would fit the rifle. Keane, the slayer, pretended that he thought Roderick was about to shoot him, yet Keane was within four or five feet of him and shot Roderick in the left side, the bullet passing through the heart, showing plainly that when Roderick received the fatal wound, he was not at all facing Keane, and could not have been making or attempting to make an assault upon Keane that he claims.

Another peculiar matter about the slaying of Roderick is that one of the mine owners, a gentleman by the name of Graham, who went with Keane down the road to meet Roderick, claiming that they believed Roderick to have been guilty sometime last summer of having held up their Treasurer and robbed him of bullion amounting to something like ten thousand dollars, but seeing Roderick coming, he, Graham, hid behind a stump and remained there until after Keane killed Roderick. Roderick was well knwon in the Camp, and the miners with one exception have given statements to the effect that he was always peaceable and law-abiding, sober and industrious. Roderick in his life time knew, of course, of the alleged robbery of the Treasurer of the Company. He also knew before leaving Seattle to go back there the last time that detectives had been watching him, and had been told that he was suspected. Notwithstanding all this, he pursued his business in the ordinary manner and returned openly, having announced before going that he would go to Camp McKinney on private business, a business which he had corresponded about before going.

The money which Mr. Roderick had can be accounted for, and we after looking into the matter are of the opinion that Mr. Roderick did not commit the robbery, and we are of the positive opinion, and now say that there is not in existence any tangible or reliable proof, either circumstantial or positive, that would convict Mathew Roderick with the alleged robbery.

Mr. Conway on his return reports to us that it is the uniform belief among the people and miners that he met at Camp McKinney that this killing of Roderick was unwarranted and that Keane should be punished. He was informed of this by the policeman who patroled the boundary line. He was also told by other officers and business men with whom he came in contact the same thing.

Under these circumstances, it seems to us that the ends of justice demand that there should be a most thorough and searching investigation made, and if the information which is in our possession is true in the material particulars, this man Keane should be dealt with according to law, and any way that he should not be allowed to go at large until he is discharged by a competent tribunal, after having a thorough investigation in your Courts. We are informed that you are the proper person to whom we should make these representations, and that you are a gentleman who will see that justice is done.

If we can be of any further assistance to you, or if Mrs. Roderick can, you have only to request it.

Very respectfully submitted,
Brady & Gay.

BIBLIOGRAPHY

BOOKS
Adnay, Tppan. *The Klondike Stampede.* New York and London: Harper and Brothers Publishers, 1900.
Akrigg, G.P.V. and Helen B. *1001 British Columbia Place Names.* Vancouver: Discovery Press, 1973.
Attwood, Mae. *Border Gold.* Grand Forks Gazette Printing Co. Ltd., 1981.
Bancroft, Hubert H. *History of British Columbia 1792-1887.* San Francisco: The History Company, 1887.
Barlee, N.L. *Gold Creeks and Ghost Towns.* Summerland: Canada West Magazine, 1980.
Basque, Garnet: *Methods of Placer Mining.* Langley: Sunfire Enterprises Ltd., 1983.
Berton, Pierre. *Klondike.* Toronto: McClelland & Stewart, 1958.
Howay, F.W., and Scholefield, E.V.S. *British Columbia Historical.* Toronto: The S.J. Clarke Publishing Co., 1914.
Hughes, Katherine. *Father Lacombe: The Black-Robe Voyageur.* New York: Moffat, Yard and Co., 1914.
Kelly, L.V. *The Range Men.* Toronto: Coles Publishing Co. Ltd., 19 .
Lawrence, J.C. *Brief History of Sooke District.*
Lindquist, H.L., ed. *The Stamp Specialist.* New York: H.L. Lindquist, 1945.
Martinsen, Ella L. *Black Sand and Gold.* Portland: Binford & Mort, Publishers, 1983.
————. *Trail to North Star Gold.* Portland: Binford & Mort, Publishers, 1974.
Moore, J. Bernard. *Skagway in Days Primeval.* New York: Vantage Press, 1968.
Nicholson, George. *Vancouver Island's West Coast 1792-1962.*
Ogilvie, William. *Early Days on the Yukon.* Toronto: John Lane Company, 1913.
Paterson, T.W. *Ghost Towns of the Yukon.* Langley: Stagecoach Publishing Co. Ltd., 1977.
Patterson, R.M. *The Dangerous River.*
Riley, Dan, Primrose, Tom and Dempsey, Hugh. *The Lost Lemon Mine.* Surrey: Frontier Books, 1980.
Walbran, Capt. John T. *British Columbia Coast Names.* Vancouver: J.J. Douglas Ltd., 1971.

NEWSPAPERS AND MAGAZINES
Alberta Historical Review.
Boundary Historical Report.
B.C. Digest.
B.C. Historical Quarterly.
B.C. Minister of Mines Report.
Canada West.
Canadian Frontier.
Canadian West.
Grand Forks *Miner.*
Helena *Daily Herald.*
The Mining Record.
New Westminster *British Columbian.*
The Shoulder Strap.
Similkameen Star.
Vancouver *Province.*
Victoria *Colonist.*
Victoria *Times*

INDEX